When You Come Together

When You Come Together serves as an important discussion partner for the issues faced in the contemporary church. It is an innovative book filled with practical examples of how to make worship relevant to the 21st century. Amy Anderson's thought provoking treatment of the terms pentecostal and charismatic will be a helpful corrective to the division that all too often centers around them. Anyone interested in the health of the church and seeing it achieve its highest potential will benefit greatly from this book.

> Thomas A. Vollmer, PhD Candidate Katholieke Universiteit Leuven
> Minister and former missionary to Belgium

When You Come Together is definitely a great book. I honestly discovered new insights and inspiration toward becoming a more Biblically grounded effective pastor, leader, servant and member of the Body of Christ. I highly recommend that you read, make practical applications, and pass Amy's book on to your best friends!

> Walt Kallestad
> Community Church of Joy
> ReignDown USA
> Author of *Everday Anytime Prayer, The Everyday, Anytime Guide to Christian Leadership,* and other books, including co-author of *The Passionate Life.*

For those who are hungry for significant encounters with God when they gather for worship, *When You Come Together* provides crystal clear biblical wisdom as well as constructive community skills, empowering God's people to create a gathering that is both biblical and uniquely their own.

> Dr Anita Koeshall
> Director of Students for Christ-Europe
> Cross-cultural trainer

When You Come Together

Challenging the Church to an
Interactive Relationship with God

Amy S. Anderson

Being Church

When You Come Together

© 2010, Amy Anderson

ISBN 978-0-9829010-0-7

Being Church
www.beingchurch.com

Excerpts from the New Testament are original translations by the author.

Scripture references marked NASB are taken from the NEW AMERICAN STANDARD BIBLE®, Copyright © 1960, 1962, 1963, 1968, 1971, 1972, 1973, 1975, 1977, 1995 by The Lockman Foundation. Used by permission.

Cover design by Jon Wilcox, www.grandemporiumdesign.com

Printed in the United States of America

Table of Contents

Acknowledgements

By the time that you have read through a chapter or so of *When You Come Together*, you will come to recognize that this book was written by a village, the community of believers who have been part of my life since childhood, who have discipled me, encouraged me, corrected me, and taught me to expect more.

A few members of my "village" who stand out in relation to the topic of this book are Jim Bradford, whose inspired leadership of Christians In Action University Church in the 1970s and 80s opened my eyes to the possibility that a group of believers could seek the presence of God and respond to His voice; my valiant student leaders in Students For Christ-Koeln who not only believed that we could reach the heart of God together but often got there ahead of me; and the leadership team of St Stephens Church, who taught me that it is possible for a Spirit-guided team to lead a congregation without power struggles.

Later village members have actively participated in the writing of this book. Over the years of teaching the *Community of Worship and Prayer* course at North Central University, I asked my students to write their own thoughts in the margins of early drafts of *When You Come Together*. Those whose comments are included are (in no particular order) Dan, Bree, John, Jared, Stacey, Chris, Jennifer,

Acknowledgements

Kris, Nikki, Matt, Heather, Aaron, Jessie, Jim, and Annie.[1] Their passionate desire to experience the reality of God made it possible for the small community we built each semester to interact with God through His very present Holy Spirit.

Several ministry colleagues, some of whom also took the class in the early years before a manuscript existed, have commented on the later stages of *When You Come Together*. These are Anita, Mike, Chuck, Sally, Phil, Carina, Danielle, Ashok, Tim, and Blake.[2]

Several wise, articulate, and experienced mentors have read and commented on the entire manuscript. Tom Vollmer, Anita Koeshall, Matt Wolf, and Tim Enloe encouraged, corrected, explored ideas, and assisted with the organization of the document.

Final details of the manuscript, such as the bibliography, index, and fact-checking, were conscientiously worked through by the eagle eyes of Mike Newland, Jon Fulk, and Sara Ellingsworth. Any mistakes that remain are my very own.

I entered into the adventure of self-publishing with some trepidation, but was fortunate to be connected to Chris MacKinnon, who designed, formatted, and guided me through the publication process. Similarly, Jon Wilcox patiently interacted with me on cover design, with many back-and-forth responses until we had it right.

---

[1] When you see these names in the short comments, you should imagine a 20-something in the middle of his/her BA degree at a Christian university.

[2] When you see their names, you should imagine experienced campus missionaries who have been living out the possibilities I describe.

*How should it be then, brothers
and sisters? It should be like this:
When you come together, each of you
brings something to share. Here are
examples: A psalm, a teaching, a
revelation, a message in an unknown
language, an interpretation of that
message. Everything that happens in
the gathering should be for the
building up of the whole body.*

1 Corinthians 14:26

Introduction

What is the meaning of church? Do we come together to offer praise? To hear instruction? To entertain the "audience of One?" To pay our tithes and offerings? To pray for each other? To plan social events or work toward social justice? To evangelize the lost?

Why do Christians come together?

For years, I taught a college course called *Community of Worship and Prayer*. The foundations for this course were laid in my early ministry years in the Upper Midwest and Germany, during which I observed, participated in, and eventually led groups of believers who truly intended to meet with and hear from God in a way that is foreign to many Western Christians today. Having experienced what a depth of relationship can be the norm between God and the people of God, I was sad that so many believers never even dream that it is possible. When I returned to the US and began postgraduate studies at Fuller Seminary, I purposely took extra ecclesiology courses that allowed me to "theologize" about the significant encounters with God that had occurred over those years. My ministry experiences, my studies, and the enthusiastic

> *Theology.* Most precisely a study of God and God's relation to the world, but often also used to speak of a person's entire religious system of thinking.
>
> *Christology.* A study of Jesus, the Christ or Messiah, His identity, His person, and His works.
>
> *Pneumatology.* A study of the Holy Spirit, His identity, His person, and His works.
>
> *Ecclesiology.* A study of the church, its purpose and meaning.

response of my students in the *Community* class have led to the creation of the book you are about to read.

In the earlier semesters of teaching the *Community* course, I spoke in terms of developing a *theology of worship.* However, we found that the word "worship" is too limited in current usage—basically understood as the song-singing part of a church "service." As the course developed over the years, we began to center our discussion more in aspects of ecclesiology—in particular an understanding of the meaning of the church gathering. In the process, we wandered into some of the other "-ologies" as well.

Rather than using the term *ecclesiology,* which is broader than our focus here, I've begun to use a more limited expression; a *theology of the gathered people of God,* and to encourage my

> Bree: "I like 'gathering' better than 'church.' It doesn't bring in negative connotations."

students to explore the more specific question of what happens, or ought to be happening, at Christian gatherings.

When You Come Together is not a complete, and certainly not a systematic, ecclesiology. There are huge, vital, important things that we will not discuss. I will not be expanding on the mission of the church, for example, even though this aspect of ecclesiology is essential to the identity and purpose of the people of God, and should be an immediate result of our gatherings. There are also significant theological discussions to be had concerning salvation, Christology, and so on.

For the purposes of this book, I am more concerned with those doctrinal understandings that affect our faith life in immediate ways. That is not to say that other theological pursuits are not valid and valuable. It simply recognizes that our discussion has had limitations placed on it in order to keep it simple and practical.

I do hope, at the same time, to raise issues you may not have thought about, and to start you on the road to developing a vital biblical theology of the gathered people of God. If you grab hold of the essence of what it means for God's people to gather, and go

> Aaron: "As much as we know intellectually about worship, we must have heart knowledge."

beyond an intellectual agreement to practical expression, you will begin to reflect good theology through your own healthy participation in community life.

You will find discussion questions, as well as a few exercises, interspersed throughout the book. You are certainly free to ignore them. You are also welcome to do them on your own. However, they are meant to be done together in a community setting, perhaps a Bible study, home group, or leadership team. One central point of *When You Come Together* is that church is not program but family, and the discussion questions are meant to help you work towards the realization of that goal. Let's try one right now:

Reflect: As you prepare to read farther, what thoughts or questions are in your mind? Do you already have strong opinions about the church gathering? Or is this a whole new line of thought for you? What do you think I meant when I said that church is not program but family?

The Gathering
of Believers

"WE are the New Testament church!" "No, WE are!"

As far as I am aware, every Christian group claims to find
support for their vision of ministry and their ecclesiastical structure
in the pages of the Bible. Yet if the Catholics and the Baptists, the
Methodists and the Church of
God in Christ, the Mennonites and
the Presbyterians all earnestly call
themselves "the New Testament
Church," then either one group is correct and all the others have
missed the boat (and there are those who would make such a
claim), or else the scripture is far less explicit on most of these
issues than a lot of us would like to admit.

> John: "We the church tend to take
> pride in and worship our beliefs
> and doctrines over our God."

Healthy Use of Scripture

One of the questions we are going to explore is, "What does the
Bible say about the church?" For that reason, it would be good to
spend a few minutes on the purpose and use of scripture. We tend
to read the *books* of the Bible as if they were chapters in one large
document, which we also call a *book*. And, as a matter of fact, *book*

is not a bad designation for Exodus, Isaiah, Mark, or I Thessalonians, since each section of the Bible was originally written as a separate document, for a specific audience in a specific situation.

Scholars often call the books of the Bible *occasional* literature. Something happened (an occasion) to cause each document to be written. The prophet Haggai felt constrained by God to speak out about the decadence and sinfulness of Israel. The author of the Gospel of John found it necessary to write to his congregation with a treatise about Jesus that would encourage their faith in a difficult situation. The apostle Paul was so upset that he was moved to strong words when he heard that the Christians in Galatia were on the verge of giving up the freedom of the gospel for the slavery of legalism.

And so they wrote. We thank God for the situations that caused them to write, because the biblical documents give us a window into the Jewish backgrounds and early stages of the Christian faith. But that is not all. The collected books of the Bible have been recognized as the revelation of God to the people of God in all places and generations. The words of scripture are eternal and do not fail to achieve this revelatory purpose. They still give life and guidance to us, who live 2000 years later in an entirely different culture.

The distance of time and culture, however, challenges us to learn how to interpret and apply the teachings of the Bible faithfully and correctly. If the earliest Christian documents were written to a specific situation, then they have a liveliness and vitality that we often miss when we attempt to read scripture as if it were a theology book. This is about real people in real historical situations. So if we want to understand the books of the Bible, we need to work at understanding the time and place for which they were originally written. [3]

In that case...

The goal of this book is to guide you and me into a healthy understanding of the gathering of believers, which English-speaking people normally call *church*. So, let's turn to our Bibles. What is the first thing we learn about the church when we read the earliest Christian documents?

Study: If you are the sort of person who likes to do his/her own thinking, I have an exercise for you to do before you read farther. Better yet, do this as a group exercise.

Sit down with your New Testament and skim through at least one Gospel and all the rest (Acts, the Epistles, the Revelation). As you read, take note of every instance that provides us with a glimpse into the first-century gatherings of believers. Try very hard not to read your 21st century assumptions and experiences back into the text.

Here are some questions that may be helpful:

How many churches were in that city?
How often did they meet?
On what day?
At what time?
Where did they meet?
How many people gathered at one place?
Did all the Christians meet together or were they scattered in
*   smaller house churches?*
What structure(s)—if any—may have been the norm?
What did they do when they met?
Who was at the meetings?

---

[3] If you would like to know more about proper use of scripture, see the book by Fee and Stuart, listed in the bibliography.

What were they doing well? What not so well?
Who did they understand themselves to be?

After you finish reading and taking notes, draw some conclusions and write those out as well. Discuss them together before reading further.

The New Testament Church

I don't know about you, but the first thing I notice when I search the New Testament is that there has never been a *perfect* church. We cannot hold up the first-century church as a role model

for how Christians ought to behave. They squabbled over trivial matters while ignoring gross sin in their midst. They were easily led

> Chris: *"Often people point to the 1st century church as the role model, thinking that if we could just become like it, there would be the perfect church."*

astray into both *legalism* and *libertinism*.[4] They were arrogant, stubborn, weak-kneed, and unstable. Pagan influences caused gentile Christians to be susceptible to false teaching, while wrong-headed Jewish Christians argued that people could not be disciples of Jesus unless they kept the entire ritual law.

---

[4] In the Christian context, *legalism* is the tendency to want to have your whole life determined by rules. There is a kind of security in having everything laid out for you. And then you can judge everyone else who doesn't follow your rules. The opposite is *libertinism*, which would be a tendency to say that since we are saved by grace, it doesn't matter how we behave. God loves us anyway. Well God does provide us with a few necessary laws to help us know right from wrong, but He also gives us the law of love, and the Holy Spirit to live within us and teach us how to make decisions on the questions that are not so obvious.

Even being so close to the time of Jesus and led by the apostles who were personally touched by Him, 1st century churches were no closer to the ideal than we are today.

Secondly, when we look to the New Testament for a pattern to follow, we quickly recognize that there is no clear *church structure* in the New Testament. There is actually very little description of church gatherings at all, and what is described seems to vary from city to city. We are forced to read between the lines to discern things that will help us develop and strategize today. Indeed, we must learn to ask more searching questions. For example:

> *What was the self-understanding (theology) that developed in the churches as a result of the apostles' earliest teachings? Such understanding is, to a large extent, taken for granted in the New Testament writings.*

> *How did the authors of scripture attempt to correct churches that had gone astray? What can we learn about God's intention for the church from these corrections?*

Just as we cannot look to the first-century church to find a role model church, neither can we look to the early church fathers or to any later denominational/institutional developments to find a church that is exactly (or even nearly) a representation of what Jesus intends. Church structure, methodology, and eccesiology, are always human constructions. At their best, they are the result of people trying very hard to hear from God, and prayerfully applying good theology to their cultural settings. But building the church has never been an exact science.

So, search as you may, you are not going to find, nor are you going to build, the perfect church. However, if God's people study, pray, and consider carefully, we will find principles in scripture that can open a window to the wise intentions of God, and help us to be faithful followers as we build up the church together.

Reflect: Does the lack of exacting instructions for how the church should be make you feel insecure, or does it make you feel more free? What changes could this new awareness bring about in your thinking and behavior?

Words change their meaning

There are several terms that we should discuss at this point. These words have their roots in scripture, and ought to be helpful in understanding the church. However, Western culture and the English language have caused them to develop meanings that have strayed somewhat from the intention of scripture.

Believe. Americans tend to understand the word group that is translated *believe/belief/faith* to mean *intellectual assent.* "I believe" in our society means something like "I agree," or "I affirm that it is true." However, if you look at the Hebrew basis for this word group (and the writers of the New Testament documents are steeped in Hebrew thought patterns), you will find that it is much more about relationship, and in particular about trust.

When scripture challenges us to "have faith" or to "believe," it is not that we are expected to work up some sort of confident expectation, or to simply agree to a creed. Instead it is a challenge to *trust* in God, to *surrender* to Him, to stop worrying, to proclaim that only God has the answers, the power, the wisdom for our situation. *I believe* means *I trust You because I know You.*

Corporate. Don't think in terms of a corporation—like a company. Think of the older meaning of this word—which has to do with the *body.* When we talk about the corporate gathering of believers, we mean that we are the body of Christ, the physical revelation of who God is.

You. The Bible nearly always speaks in the *second person plural.* Don't remember your English grammar? Well, the second person in English is *you.* Problem is, we use the same word for both the singular and plural forms of the second person. If I say "You are the best," I might mean just you—that one person who is reading this sentence. Or I might mean—as southern-state Americans are able to say—"you all"—the whole group of you to whom I am referring.

Very little in scripture is spoken/written to one individual person. When you see the English word *you* in the New Testament, the Greek is normally in the second person plural, referring to a group of people. Why is this important? Because we Americans have tended to read the Bible as if it were

> *Jared: "Until we are concerned about our brothers and sisters, we will never grow."*

addressed to individuals, each of us privately pursuing our own relationship to God. However, both the ancient cultures and the ancient languages make it clear that God is calling a *people,* speaking to us collectively, and seeing us not so much as individuals, but as a coordinated body made of many unique and indispensable parts.

Worship. A wonderful word that means "to ascribe worth." We definitely want to do that to God. But, in our culture, worship has become limited to the singing part of our gatherings. Is singing to and

> *Mike: "Worship is a continual awareness of the presence of the glory of God."*

about God the only way to worship? We will work on unpacking this word throughout the book.

Church Service. Hmm. I don't really like this term. I'm sure that when Christians started using this word to describe their gatherings, they meant that they wanted to serve God in their coming together, that worship is a spiritual service. Romans 12:1-2, for example, relates worship to the OT idea of offering a sacrifice (expanded on in the rest of the chapter) and calls it a spiritual act of service.

But in current American culture, attending a "service" carries the connotation of attending a program. It certainly describes the reality—we typically do attend a program every Sunday morning. But is that really what we want? Is that what God intended? Maybe we should stop using the word *service* to describe a gathering of believers. Maybe that would assist us in moving away from the tendency to want to "put on a show" on Sunday mornings?

> Chris: "Yes! I'm sick of services!"

These definitions can help us more nearly approach a scriptural understanding of the gathering of believers, and aid in our continuing discussion. In the next chapter, we will explore two other important terms—*pentecostal* and *charismatic*—terms that are often loaded with unnecessary baggage. Let's try and recover what they *ought* to mean.

Reflect: Share your thoughts about the terms defined above, as well as any other "church" terminology that, in your opinion, is filled with unintended baggage or frequently misunderstood.

Pentecostal and Charismatic

Whoa, you say, I'm not one of those. Or, on the other hand, you may be thinking of skipping this section since you already have a clear picture of what these terms signify. I'd like to challenge us all to look again, and to at least for the moment leave aside the cultural definitions that these words carry in America today.

What Should We Mean When We Call Ourselves Pentecostal?

The term comes, of course, from the Day of Pentecost, a day that has huge significance for all followers of Jesus. Pentecost is a Jewish feast day that occurs 50 days after Passover, and it was on this day of celebration that God chose to pour out the Holy Spirit on the first disciples of Jesus. Pentecost was the day the church was born.

So, one way to see the term *pentecostal* is as a description of all believers. If you follow Jesus, you are part of the movement that began on the Day of Pentecost, and therefore you may call yourself a pentecostal.[5] However, I'd like to take this a bit further by exploring why some Christians chose to name themselves *"Pentecostals"* at the beginning of the 20th century. We will see that they had good reason to do this, although many of their spiritual children, even if they still call themselves Pentecostal 100 years later, may no longer qualify.

The pattern of Pentecost

Here's what happened on the day the church was born. After He rose from the dead, Jesus spent 40 days with His followers. Then, just before ascending into heaven, He instructed them to wait until they received some sort of visitation of power that would make them able to be witnesses to the world. The disciples were obedient. They found a room big enough for all of them— 120 men and women—and they stayed there and waited and prayed and expected.

Did they know what they were waiting for? Did they know what was going to happen? Not at all. But they trusted Jesus and turned their hearts toward Him. They waited and expected.

Then came the astonishing and overwhelming act of God upon the gathered believers. The sounds, the sights, and the physical responses in their bodies were a surprise, and far beyond what they could ever have imagined. God acted sovereignly upon His faithful gathered people by pouring out His Holy Spirit.

———————————

[5] For the purposes of this book, I will differentiate between *pentecostal* (with a small "p"), meaning people or churches that fulfill the definition of *pentecostal* that I am developing here, and Pentecostal (with a capital "P"), meaning people or churches that take their name from the Pentecostal movement that started in the early 20th century.

> When the time arrived for the Day of Pentecost, they were
> all together in the same place. Suddenly a roar came out
> of heaven. It was like a violent driving wind and it filled
> the whole house where they were sitting. What appeared
> to them then were tongues, as if of fire, being distributed,
> and they rested upon each one of them. They were all
> filled with the Holy Spirit and began to speak in other
> languages,[6] as the Spirit gave them ability to speak.[7]

Notice what happens next. The response of the 120 could have been self-centered. They could have made their meeting room into a sort of shrine to honor this marvelous day, and kept the blessing to themselves. But instead, barely able to control themselves, laughing, dancing, worshiping God, prophesying, and speaking in languages they'd never learned, the men and women poured out onto the street. They soon drew a crowd, and the crowd was so intrigued by the supernatural manifestations that they listened attentively to Peter's explanation of what this was all about.[8]

---

[6] The Greek word used for this manifestation of the Holy Spirit is "tongues." What it means is a language that the person receiving and speaking it has never learned.

[7] Whenever you see a quotation from the New Testament in this book, it is my own translation. I've tried to aim for accessible language while staying faithful to the intention of the text. All quotes of the Old Testament are from the New American Standard Bible.

[8] Tim Enloe, who generously reviewed and commented on the entire book manuscript, pointed out that there are differing reconstructions of the location(s) of the believers on the Day of Pentecost. Some commentators argue that the coming of the Spirit must have been in the temple/temple courts. For example, the last verses of Luke's Gospel, as well as Acts 2 & 4 tell us that the disciples continued to meet in the temple. In addition, it is a major pilgrimage feast, so wouldn't they be at the temple during the day? → On the other hand, it was only 9 in the morning when the wind came, and Acts reports that the wind filled the whole *house* where they were *sitting*. But then where did the thousands of bystanders come from? One possible solution is that they moved from the house to the temple. Or that they were able to draw

Now there were godly Jewish men living in Jerusalem,
from all the nations under heaven. When the noise
started, a crowd gathered, bewildered because each of
them could hear them speaking in his own dialect. They
were amazed. They marveled. They said, "Aren't all
these people from Galilee? So how can it be that each of us
hears them in our mother-tongue?" (There were Parthians
and Medes and Elamites and people from Mesopotamia,
Judea, Cappadocia, Pontus, Asia, Phrygia, Pamphylia,
Egypt, and the areas of Libya around Cyrene. There were
visitors from Rome—both Jews and converts to Judaism—
as well as Cretans and Arabs.) They said, "We hear these
people speaking the great deeds of God in our own
languages!" And they were all astonished and wondered
aloud, "What is going on here?" But some mocked them
and said, "They've had too much new wine."

What did Peter see?

What happened on the Day of Pentecost was certainly
meaningful and wonderful. Members of Pentecostal churches are
right to point out that when God poured out the Holy Spirit there
was visible and audible evidence, including speaking in unknown
languages. But sometimes we fail to see the forest for the trees.
Let's read on.

Peter, however, stood up with the eleven, shouted, and
proclaimed to them, "Men of Judea and all you inhabitants
of Jerusalem, pay attention! Mark my words! These
people are not drunk, though it might appear so to you.

---

such a crowd in front of the house because so many were in the streets,
headed to the temple for the celebration.

After all, it is only 9.00 in the morning. No, rather this is what the prophet Joel was talking about when he said:

'God says, "This is what it will be like in the last days. I will pour out from my Spirit on all people, and your sons and your daughters will prophesy. Your young men will see visions and the elders among you will have dreams. Indeed, in the last days I will pour out from my Spirit on both my male and female servants, and they will prophesy."'"

You just read that Peter looked around at the astonishing things that were happening and was led to think of a passage from the prophet Joel. There were other texts that he could have quoted instead. The Hebrew Bible contains numerous prophecies about God's desire and plan to send the Spirit, to send renewal so that His people would have hearts of flesh instead of stone, to write His law on their hearts.[9] What was it that caused Peter to think of *Joel's* prophecy rather than any of the others that would have seemed just as fitting?

Almost certainly the aspect of God's action that impacted Peter most was not *what* was happening, but *to whom* it was happening.

What they expected

Just a few days before, as the 120 disciples were waiting in the rented room, it was Peter himself who had led the group in drawing lots for a person to replace Judas, who had betrayed Jesus and committed suicide. It seems that the expectation of the disciples before Pentecost was that Jesus was going to use a hand-picked group of 12 Jewish men as the leaders of His coming

---

[9] For example, Isaiah 44:3-5; 59:21; Ezekiel 36:26-27; 37:14; 39:29; and Zephaniah 3:9.

kingdom. This is pretty much in line with the Old Testament norm that the Spirit of God would come upon an elite group of Jewish men (such as the judge, [10] prophet,[11] priest, or king). Peter and the others seem to have been convinced that Judas needed to be replaced so that the symbolic number of 12 Jewish men would be full again. Surely these 12 would represent the 12 tribes of Israel and be the key players in the new kingdom.

If you had asked them ahead of time, almost certainly the first followers of Jesus would have expected God to differentiate between the Twelve and all the other disciples. According to the only pattern they knew so far, the Spirit should have been poured out exclusively on the 12 male leaders.

What really happened

But did the Spirit come on only the Twelve? No, on all those present. Perhaps the Spirit came more strongly on the Twelve? No, all received the same gift. Surely then it was only men who received? No, both men and women. In fact, it is probably the gender issue that leads Peter to Joel's prophecy—"On your sons *and daughters*....your servants *and maidservants*...." At Pentecost, God was truly doing a new thing, a radical thing. Not only the elite, not only the men, and soon it would be clear that it was not only the Jews. All nations and races, all economic and social statuses, both genders. Everyone who trusts Jesus can receive the blessing of the Holy Spirit.

---

[10] With the notable exception of Deborah (Judges 4 and 5).
[11] And don't forget Huldah (II Kings 22).

Pentecost keeps happening

Acts goes on to describe other examples of experiences that follow this pentecostal pattern.   God acted sovereignly and surprisingly on earnest gatherings of seekers, and those seekers responded by embracing the new thing God was doing.   Here are some of the most central examples.

Paul's conversion

Paul, driven by his zeal for God's honor and what he thought was correct theology, was busy trying to exterminate those heretics who claimed that Jesus of Nazareth was the Messiah.   Though Paul was dead wrong in his desire to please God, he was dead earnest, truly trying to do God's work.

Reflect: Have you, like Paul, ever found yourself fighting against God even though you wanted to please Him?

Jesus met Paul sovereignly and unexpectedly during a journey to Damascus, knocking him off his donkey and blinding him. Then, having gotten his attention, Jesus introduced Himself to Paul personally.   On the basis of that encounter, Paul entered into a trust relationship with Jesus and obeyed Jesus' instructions to go into the city and wait.   Do you notice how this fits the pentecostal pattern?   An earnest (if wrong-headed) seeker, a sovereign act of God, the human embrace of that unexpected divine act.

There followed a pentecostal revelation to Ananias, a follower of Jesus, who—against his better judgment—also trusted Jesus' surprising instruction in a vision and was obedient to visit Paul. Paul could have rejected God's initiative both on the road and through Ananias, but he responded with humility.   The result is the miraculous healing and initial mentoring of the man who would soon cause the gospel to break out of its Jewish bounds and turn the world upside down.

Outsiders receive the Spirit

Then there are the times when the gospel is taken to the followers of John the Baptist and to the Samaritans. In both cases, groups of people who were earnestly seeking God received further revelation and responded willingly to the surprising news that Jesus was the way to life for them as well. These new believers experienced supernatural manifestations of the Spirit similar to those that occurred on the Day of Pentecost.

Peter, Cornelius, and the Gentiles

But the most powerful scriptural example of a pentecostal experience is surely God's visitation to Peter and to Cornelius. Both men were earnestly seeking God, both received a surprising visit from God, and when they embraced God's revelation, the result was truly astonishing.

Cornelius had long been a *God-fearer*, a gentile man who worshiped the God of the Jews but did not fully convert to the Jewish faith and obey the whole ritual law, including circumcision. He was not alone in his faith walk. Cornelius was surrounded by members of his own household and many friends who were seeking and worshipping God with him. One day, while Cornelius was praying, this earnest openness to God was rewarded with a sudden visitation—a vision of an angel who gave them the surprising instructions to find Peter and bring him to meet them.

Meanwhile, Peter, who was praying and fasting some distance away, also received a vision in which it was made clear to him that God is able to call something clean that Peter had always understood to be unclean. Then he was given instructions to cooperate with some gentiles who had been sent to fetch him—

something he would not otherwise have been willing to do. Gentiles are, after all, unclean!

When Peter arrived at Cornelius' home, he recognized that something was afoot, and figured the best thing would be to tell these folks the same story about Jesus that he'd told on the Day of Pentecost. But before he'd even adequately explained the gospel, the gentiles received the same outpouring of the Holy Spirit and the same manifestations of joyful adoration, prophesying, and speaking in unknown languages.

Peter recognized that this was a sovereign act of God. Even though it seemed to contradict everything he'd ever thought about the differences between Jews and gentiles, he was sensitive enough to the Holy Spirit to embrace it.

He baptized them.

Unheard of! He baptized uncircumcised heathens! Didn't he know that only Jews could become followers of the Messiah?!

Peter was soon called on the carpet for this act, and his explanation to the other leaders is a classical pentecostal statement:

> "As I began to speak, the Holy Spirit fell upon them, just as He did upon us at the beginning. And I remembered the word of the Lord, how He used to say, 'John baptized with water, but you shall be baptized with the Holy Spirit.' If God therefore gave to them the same gift that He gave to us after we trusted in the Lord Jesus as Messiah, who was I that I could stand in God's way?"
> (Acts 11:15-17)

Who was I that I could stand in God's way?

The Pentecostal pattern

Let us distill the events down to what I'm going to call "the pentecostal pattern." The pattern is:

1 – A believer or group of believers earnestly seeks God.

2 – God acts sovereignly and surprisingly on them.

3 – They respond to God's unexpected initiative with what we might call a Holy Spirit-guided embrace—a humble obedience in spite of the newness of what God is doing. The result is often the formation of something entirely outside the box.

So who is a pentecostal?

A pentecostal is someone who believes that God continues to interact with people in supernatural, personal, and unexpected ways. God is not silent, but speaks through various means, and wishes to form real corporate relationships with those who follow His Son, Jesus. Pentecostals understand God to be always speaking, always acting, always initiating new things. And they are people who will recognize the action of God, respond in trusting obedience, and humbly say, *Who are we that we could stand in God's way?*

Reflect: According to this definition, would you call yourself a pentecostal? Talk about ways in which you expect God to speak in your life and your church. Have you ever experienced that God acted sovereignly and surprisingly on a gathering of believers?

A more recent Pentecost

There have been events that echo this pentecostal pattern throughout church history. I'm sure that you can find many examples, especially at the beginnings of most movements and denominations. But I'd like us now to look at the events that led to the "Pentecostal movement," and resulted in such church groups as Pentecostal Holiness, Church of God in Christ, Assemblies of

God, and Foursquare Gospel.[12] For the sake of brevity I will be summarizing, but if you would like to learn more about this fascinating period of church history, look in the bibliography for some great reading.

In the late 1800s there arose a movement of Christians who are often referred to by the designation, "the Holiness Movement." These people earnestly sought an experience with the Holy Spirit that would allow them a sort of breakthrough to a new level of sanctified, or holy, living. Some even believed that you could pray through until God would give you total sanctification so that you would never sin again. Many people were spending hours, nights, even weeks in prayer and fasting, and they were indeed having real experiences of God that resulted in the ability to live a holy (though perhaps not sinless) life.

Some began to pay closer attention to the description in Acts 2 of the events that occurred at the birth of the church—back on that first Day of Pentecost. They noticed that the first believers experienced some marvelous things like uncontainable joy and the ability to prophesy, to speak in unknown languages, and to powerfully spread the good news about Jesus. They realized that even though they were finding help from the Holy Spirit in their goal to live holy lives, they weren't experiencing these other things.

So quite a few Holiness Christians began seeking what they often called the "third work of the Holy Spirit" (after salvation and sanctification). They studied scripture, prayed and fasted, and gathered with other people who were waiting and expecting God to act.

---

[12] Please be aware that I am describing only the American version of the beginning of the Pentecostal movement. Similar occurrences happened all over the world at around the same time. Pentecost is not a uniquely American experience. Far from it.

Did God choose the date on purpose or could it have been any day? I don't know. But on New Year's Day 1901—the first day of the new century—at about 7.00 p.m., a young woman named Agnes Osman prayed in a language she had never learned.[13] This became the most publicized modern occurrence of what Pentecostals call "speaking in tongues."[14] Soon many other people were having the same experience and were encouraging everyone they met to seek God for it. In most cases these rather exuberant and annoyingly evangelistic folk were rejected by their own denominations.

They began to call themselves Pentecostals. The name is certainly fitting: These were people who had sought God earnestly for a long time. Though many church leaders of that day had taught that the manifestations of the Holy Spirit died out with the apostles, here was God, giving people these very phenomena in wild abundance. Guided by the Holy Spirit, people of like experience and vision came together in community, and a new movement began which was to be the source of the fastest growing Christian movement in the world today.

Pentecost gets even more surprising

Not only did a new movement begin, but developments within that movement were outside of the box for the theological and social backgrounds that these people came from. In a time of institutionalized racial prejudice, there were notable instances not only of blacks and whites worshiping together, but of blacks

---

[13] See Parham, p. 65, where Osman recounts the event in her own words.

[14] It was not the first modern occurrence. Tongues-speaking had occurred in Holiness circles for more than a decade. But a majority of Pentecostals point to Osman's experience as the spark that set off the movement that would follow.

leading gatherings in which white people were participants. In a time when women could not vote and were not equal under the law, Pentecostals recognized that the Spirit had been poured out on both genders without distinction. As a result, most Pentecostal denominations have ordained women to the ministry alongside men from day one.

Summary on being pentecostal

A pentecostal is a person who expects God to speak and act when the people of God gather and earnestly seek Him. And when God responds, no matter how unexpectedly, pentecostals take it seriously and obey. That's how I want to be. And I want to gather regularly with other people who want to be pentecostal.

Don't you?

> Carina: "I grew up being taught that signs and wonders were only for the apostles, but my experience with God taught me that this wasn't true. I identify as pentecostal now, and make every effort to listen to God and stay open to how the Spirit is at work around me"

What Should We Mean When We Call Ourselves Charismatic?

This is a word straight out of the original language of your New Testament. *Charis* is Greek for "grace," and the derived term *charismata* is a plural that means something like "things of grace," or "grace gifts," in other words a gift given regardless of whether the person has earned it.

In quite a few of his letters, Paul mentions grace gifts in lists. So the first thing we need to discuss is how Paul writes lists. Remember we said that the Bible is basically made up of *occasional* documents? That means that there was an historical occasion that caused the author to write. Well, another way to say that is to describe scripture as *ad hoc* literature. *Ad hoc* is a Latin phrase that translates roughly "to this," or "for this reason." We can speak of Paul's letters as being *ad hoc* because they are written for a specific reason. In the same way, the various parts of the letters, including the lists, are *ad hoc*.

This is significant because it helps us to avoid the mistake of making any of Paul's lists into some sort of final word on the subject. When Paul lists off types of sins, for example, he is not saying that there are no other sins in existence besides these. No, these are the sins he happens to think of when he writes to that particular group of people in their particular situation.

Here are a couple of sin lists. When Paul is writing to the church in Rome (13:13), he tells them how not to behave:

> *in orgies and drunkenness*
> *in extra-marital sex and indecency*
> *in strife and jealousy*

When he writes to the churches in Galatia (5:19-21), he gives them examples of "deeds of the sinful nature":

sexual immorality	*raging*
impurity	*selfish rivalries*
indecency	*dissensions*
idolatry	*factions*
witchcraft	*envy*
acts of ill will	*drunkenness*
strife	*orgies*
jealousy	

As I said, Paul also makes lists of grace gifts, or charismata. In these lists, Paul tends to provide a *mixture* of types of grace gifts — some that are supernatural, others that we are born with, others that we learn as maturing Christians. Some are leadership gifts and some are service gifts. For example, I Cor 12:28-31 includes apostles, prophets, teachers, miracles, healings, helps, administrations, and tongues, while Romans 12 includes prophecy, service, teaching, exhortation, giving, leading, and mercy.[15]

> We have different grace gifts[16] based on the grace given to us. Let's use them well. If your grace gift is prophecy, then use it as much as you have faith. The same way with grace gifts like serving others,[17] teaching, or encouraging. If your grace gift is donating, then be liberal. If it is management, do it diligently. If it is acts of mercy, do them cheerfully.
> (Romans 12:6-8)

> God placed these people in the church: first apostles, second prophets, third teachers, then miraculous acts of power, then grace gifts of healings, helpers, leadership abilities, and kinds of tongues.
> (I Corinthians 12:28)

Was Paul intending to communicate that either one of these lists is exclusive? That these are *the* gifts available to believers — no more, no less? Obviously not, since the two lists are different. Should we compile these lists and expect that every gift listed

---

[15] When you look at the context of these two lists, note that they are both located in discussions of how we are all parts of the body and we need each other.

[16] As you suspect, this is the word *charismata.*

[17] What is intended by this word in any particular context is not always clear. It can be used for service, pastoral ministry, or the office of a deacon.

somewhere in the New Testament will always be present when God's people gather? No, but it is clear that Paul expects that when believers gather, each of them will have one or more gifts that they are able to share with the body so that everyone might be built up. Read all of Romans 12 and I Corinthians 12 to get the big picture.

Reflect: Do you recognize some of these grace gifts in yourself? Do you feel that you have chances to use your grace gifts to help others?

Manifestations of the Spirit

An interesting refinement of the idea of grace gifts is the list Paul provides in I Cor 12:4-11. This is the famous list that is normally meant when people refer to the "Gifts of the Spirit," but this title is not really appropriate. The two lists that we looked at above do provide us with various examples of the charismata, and they could be titled "Some of the Grace Gifts of the Spirit."

Here, however, while Paul does start out talking more generally about different types of giftings, he gives a title to the actual list that more narrowly defines its contents. Have a look.

> There are distributions of grace gifts, but the one Spirit,
> and there are distributions of ministries, but the one Lord,
> and there are distributions of workings, but the one God,
> who works all things in all people.
>
> But to each person is given the manifestation of the Spirit
> for the benefit of all. To one person is given a word of
> wisdom by means of the Spirit. To another is given a
> word of knowledge according to the same Spirit. To
> another faith by the same Spirit, to another grace gifts of
> healings in the one Spirit, to another workings of miracles,
> to another prophecy, to another the ability to discriminate

between spirits, to another varieties of tongues, to another the ability to interpret tongues.

But all things are worked by one and the same Spirit, who distributes to each person as He sees fit.

Notice several things from this list:

1 – Paul says everyone has something of the sort listed.

2 – He says that the reason that these phenomena are given to individuals is to benefit everyone collectively.

These first two points are common to all the lists of grace gifts. The third is different:

3 – Paul does not call the items in this list *charismata*, or grace gifts, but *the manifestation of the Spirit*. The Greek word here is *phanerõsis*. This means a *revelation*, or *manifestation*—making something known.

Let's think through the whole passage together.

Paul first reminds his readers that there are many kinds of charismata, many kinds of ministries,[18] and many kinds of workings,[19] but only one Spirit/Lord/God,[20] who works all things in all people. In other words, there are a great variety of grace gifts of all types available to God's people, but God is in charge of how they are distributed and used.

Then, in verse 7, Paul says *but*. There are all sorts of grace gifts, *but* each person receives the manifestation of the Spirit for the common good. And then he follows by listing the nine

---

[18] Same word as is discussed in the previous footnote.

[19] The Greek is energeimatõn, the source of our word *energy*, and appears to refer to action type services done by gifted Christians in the church. The related verb is used when it says that God "works" all things in all people.

[20] Notice the expression of the Trinity.

manifestations with which traditional Pentecostals are familiar.[21] It seems that *grace gifts* should be understood as an umbrella term that covers all of the various kinds of giftings that God gives to people, and that one particular type of grace gifts is the *manifestation of the Spirit*.

One of the foremost works of the Holy Spirit is to reveal (or manifest) the mind and heart of God to the people of God. An important way that the Holy Spirit does this in the gathering of believers is by giving to individual people glimpses of God's opinion or God's goals for the current situation. For example, the Spirit might communicate with the church by revealing to one or more people a scripture passage, or a poem, or a picture, or a song, or an idea, or a plan.

My experience in mature congregations who are open to the manifestations of the Spirit is that there will often be a series of revelations, or manifestations, that follow a thread or a theme. This theme could be expressed in a few minutes in one gathering, or it may be something that recurs and builds over months. The intention is that those who are hearing from the Spirit would inform the whole church and that the church would respond appropriately.

> Chuck: "Our main priority in life is to discern His presence among us."

I would like to emphasize that this particular list of grace gifts is a pure list. The mixed lists that we looked at above include both natural and supernatural gifts. The manifestation list consists only of examples of supernatural revelations, things that we would not be able to do in our natural abilities. It may be a challenge to you

---

[21] As always with Paul, his list is *ad hoc*. He does not intend to imply that these are the only possible manifestations, or that all nine must always be present. They are, rather, examples of how the Holy Spirit manifests the heart of God in the gathering of believers.

to know that Paul says "to each is given" about this particular list.

Reflect: Did you know that God wants to give you supernatural manifestations? Are you willing to receive and use them in order to help other people and build up the church?

Study: You might want to read through all of Paul's letters at this point, watching not only for every instance in which he lists the grace gifts, but also for examples in which he applies the giftedness of the people of God as a solution to the church's problems. Write your own summary on the charismata before reading mine below.

Summary on the charismata

Paul writes about the grace gifts repeatedly in his attempts to straighten out problem churches. Here are the most important principles we can draw from the full context of his teachings.

- Every person is unique and indispensable—a gift to the body. Paul talks about how we are all parts of the same body and that the body can't say to one of its parts, "I don't need you." Nor can any part say, "Well, since I am not an "important" part,[22] I am not part of the body." Each person has grace gifts, ranging from natural talents to developed skills to supernatural manifestations.

- The grace gifts are not given for the benefit of the individual—though each person gains much from having and using his/her gift. The gifts are given for the common good. God's grace gifts are meant to be used, not hoarded.

---

[22] or, "the part I *wanted* to be...."

So if you do not use your gifts, you are depriving other people of something God wants to give them.

- We all have gifts, but that doesn't guarantee that our gifts will be useful. We are expected to nurture and develop our gifts. Both the natural and the supernatural gifts come to us in nascent form. I may be a natural-born musician (I am not!), but if I do not practice the scales on the piano, I will never play well. I may have received the gift of discernment of spirits, but if I do not practice using it and welcome mentoring and feedback, my gift will never become useful for the church I belong to. I may have the innate ability to lead a small group Bible study, but if I refuse to be coached as a leader I will not be able to be effective in this gifting.

- Though God gives gifts without our having done something to earn them, our character development and integrity will affect whether we can be used by God in our gifts. If I receive a word of knowledge for my church, but have been back-biting another member, or doing some other sinful behavior, it may be that people will not listen to me because my sin is blocking my connection to them. My expression of

  John: "Many people forget about God's desire for righteousness."

  God's message might even be distorted because my sin is blocking my connection to God.

- There are many kinds of gifts. Some we are born with, some we learn, and some are given supernaturally. All of these gifts are given by God and we should not be arrogant about our particular gifts. Scripture expects that all God's people will have grace gifts of various types, and be willing to share them for the common good.

Reflect: Talk about gifts you recognize in each other. Is there a gift you'd like to have or grow in?

Confess: If you realize that a character flaw is blocking your ability to be used by God, now would be a good time to make a plan to confess that to a trusted friend and strategize for change.

Is love the greatest gift?

> But you seek the greatest grace gifts and I show to you all
> a still more superior way.
> (I Corinthians 12:31)

It is common for a so-called non-charismatic[23] to look at I Cor 12-14 and say to one of his/her so-called charismatic or pentecostal friends, "You have the gift of tongues, but I have the gift of love." Meaning, of course, "I don't want to have anything to do with that spooky supernatural stuff, so I will take advantage of Paul's statement in I Corinthians 12:31, and claim love as my gift," or even, "I am more mature than you because my gift is the greatest." Seems to be a rather contradictory statement, don't you think? There are several things going on here.

> Dan: "It seems that people are picking certain gifts to fit the norms of society."

The first problem is cleared up rather easily. It is a misunderstanding of love as a gift. When Paul says at the end of

---

[23] I hope you realize by now that there is no such thing as a non-charismatic Christian, if we take the word in its most straightforward biblical sense. If you are a follower of Jesus, you have charismata (grace gifts) to share, and you are therefore a "charismatic."

chapter 12 that he will show them a superior *way*, he most certainly does not mean that he is going to argue that love is the greatest *gift*. The word charisma is not used in this phrase at all. By "superior way," Paul is setting out love as the way—in other words the *framework*—for the use of the charismata.[24]

Grace gifts are only valuable if they are used in a context of love. What is love? Well, Paul is happy to give a beautiful, challenging description of how our attitudes and actions towards other members of the family of God ought to be. Guess what? We have here another one of Paul's *ad hoc* lists! Here is how he describes love:

> It is patient.
> It is kind.
> It is not jealous.
> It is not conceited.
> It is not arrogant.
> It does not behave improperly.
> It does not strive for its own advantage.
> It is not irritable.
> It does not keep record of wrong.
> It does not rejoice in wickedness.
> It rejoices together with the truth.
> It puts up with everything.
> It believes everything.
> It hopes everything.
> It endures everything.

---

[24] Tim Enloe pointed out that the Greek word (hodos) that I have translated "way" is perhaps more correctly translated "road" or "path." So, while I am presenting love as a framework for the gifts, you may find it more helpful to talk about love as the pathway to get there, or the road we must travel on as we use the grace gifts.

With these pithy words, Paul sets the context for the use of the grace gifts in the church. The manifestation gifts, and all the grace gifts, only have value when used in the framework of love, which is shorthand for patience, kindness, and so on. Not easy, no one will perfectly achieve it, but we are all challenged to try, and to forgive.

Reflect: Which description of love from this list do you find most challenging?

The second problem is that it is difficult for believers who are not familiar with the manifestation gifts to imagine being used in them. It might be a scary, uncomfortable feeling. If you don't want the challenge of having God offer you a supernatural manifestation for the building up of the body, you could prefer to say that you will choose love as your gift. I would like to provide you with a different approach to this problem, so please keep reading.

We don't speak in tongues at our church.

The classical Pentecostal denominations tend to differentiate themselves from evangelical churches by a doctrinal statement that says something to the effect that the proof of a person being "filled with the Spirit" is that the person speaks in "tongues," that is, s/he receives from God a prayer or worship language that s/he has never learned.

You, on the other hand, may be in a church that discourages or even prohibits people from speaking in tongues in any form. Some churches teach that this practice died out with the apostles or with the formation of the canon. Some say that tongues-speaking occurs today, but should be done only in private. There have been extreme teachings in some groups that people who pray in tongues are actually allowing the devil to speak through them![25]

Praying, singing, or giving a message in an unknown language is a supernatural manifestation of the Spirit that really does happen today, and if you want to see and hear someone speaking in tongues, you should visit a church that encourages the use of tongues in public gatherings. It isn't as weird as you might imagine, and is really a useful tool in helping believers go beyond their natural abilities when they need the Spirit's help to pray and worship effectively. I will provide some guidance and ideas about using a prayer language later. But first a word to those for whom this is not a familiar practice.

Contrary to the teaching of a few extreme Pentecostal groups, the ability to speak in an unknown language is not a proof of *salvation* nor a proof of the presence of the Spirit in a believer, whatever else it may be a proof of. If you have trusted your life into Jesus' hands, you have God's Spirit dwelling in you. God's Spirit gives good gifts—grace gifts—to God's people, and tongues is just one of many gifts available to you.

At the same time, I would encourage you to be open to God's desire to continue to give gifts to you. Should we say to God, "No, I don't believe that this gift is good for me, I don't want it, take it away!"? If it is from God, and God is to be trusted with our very lives, how can we say no? How can we say that any of God's grace gifts are not good?

There may be others who have a little or even a lot of exposure to the use of tongues in worship and prayer. You may have been

---

[25] No doubt the devil could make use of tongues to confuse and mislead. Every true gift of God has its counterfeits. But if you are a person truly loving and seeking God, you have no worry that this could happen to you. And God gives the gift of discernment of spirits so the church can be assured of the source of any "manifestations" that might occur.

pushed to speak in tongues, and even tried to manufacture something that sounded like tongues. You may have prayed for years and nothing has happened—as was my experience. Relax. Talk to God about this. God is not pushy. He will let you take your time. In my experience, everyone who has asked God for the manifestation gift of praying in an unknown language has received it—some immediately, some after years of waiting.

> Carina: "I had seen some things in Pentecostal churches that I didn't feel comfortable with, things that scared me and didn't look particularly like Jesus. I had a lot of mental hurdles to clear before I was open to speaking in tongues or accepting other spiritual gifts from God."

But no, you don't have to pray in tongues in order to be pleasing to God, and if your church does not allow this practice, it can still be a "pentecostal" and "charismatic" church in the sense that we are developing in this book.

Every body of believers should be pentecostal—they should seek God, wait for God, and when God speaks or acts they should respond in trusting obedience. Every body of believers should be charismatic—they should publicly recognize that all God's people are gifted gifts to the church and encourage all these gifts to be used in appropriate ways to build up the body.

Reflect: After reading this final paragraph, how do you feel— encouraged, anxious, motivated, irritated? What do you think God is saying to you or to your church group at this time?

About Leadership

In the previous chapter, we have begun to work on an understanding of how God's people are gifted and how God loves to meet with His gathered people. You might already be thinking that it is too bad that many churches don't embrace this understanding in tangible ways. We are going to need to talk about how a group of believers can learn and grow in this area, and the topic of leadership will be very important.

Reflect: At this point on your spiritual journey, how do you understand the difference between clergy and laity, or full-time vocational pastors and church members? What questions and concerns do you have?

Liberating the Laity

Books and theologies that have focused on doing away with the clergy/laity distinction have appeared at strategic points in church history. Many revival movements have had the ministry of the laity as a centerpiece to their theology and practice. Martin Luther tried to return ministry to the people, and movements like the Quakers and Anabaptists have re-introduced this with more or less success. The early years of the Pentecostal movement witnessed many Christians who had not had formal training being gifted for and released into ministry.

In the 1970s, around the time of the charismatic awakening in the mainline churches, many good books were written on this subject, in particular several by Howard Snyder (see bibliography). More recently Greg Ogden's *The New Reformation* and Vincent Donovan's *Christianity Rediscovered* do a great job of challenging us in this area. It seems that our human tendencies toward hierarchy and control continually cause us to return to behaviors that the Holy Spirit then needs to correct in each generation.

What do we mean by "liberating the laity"? There may be some disagreement here, but basically the focus is to point out that the scripture, while clearly establishing *leadership* in the body of Christ, does not prescribe a professional paid clergy who do the actual ministry (by which we tend to mean such things as preaching, leading worship, visiting the sick, planning events, etc) while the people of God are seen as support staff at best or passive consumers at worst.

Please understand that I am not intending to argue against paying pastors and others for their ministry in the church. Any form of compensation can be entirely appropriate, whether the person is on a salary, or "raises support" like many missionaries. In fact, some churches should be ashamed of how little they pay their pastors, especially the very important children's and youth pastors who are directly impacting the future of the church.

My point will be, however, that a paid clergy might not be necessary for every church, and that it has inherent dangers that we must seek to counteract by the manner in which we talk about leadership and the ways we interact with each other in the body of Christ.

Reflect: What leadership structures have you experienced in the Christian ministries in which you have participated? Have some seemed to be more effective and/or more God-honoring than others? Have you known of a church that has managed to avoid making distinctions in pay and prestige between various members of church staff? Or distinctions between full-time and volunteer leadership?

What is Leadership For?

The most significant passage in the Bible for describing how leadership gifts are used to develop ministry in the body of Christ is in Ephesians 4. Paul begins with a metaphor that is unfamiliar to us, but he uses this picture in a number of his letters, so it would be good for us to understand it.

> But grace is given to each of us, according to the measure of the gift of Messiah.[26] That's why it says, "After ascending into the high place, he took captivity captive; he gave gifts to the people."
>
> But when it says that he went up, what can that mean except that he also went down into the lower parts of the

---

[26] You will notice that I frequently use the word *Messiah* rather than the more familiar *Christ*. By this usage, I am hoping to help us to become more aware that *Christ* is not Jesus' "second name," but His title. Both Messiah (from the Hebrew) and Christ (from the Greek) mean "anointed one." The Messiah was a figure in Jewish scripture who was expected to come and bring about the "Day of the Lord," which for the Jews of Jesus' day meant release from Roman oppression. Jesus' earliest followers (all of whom were Jews) suspected and then recognized Him as Messiah, eventually realizing that the release He brought was from the captivity of sin rather than the captivity of Rome. By using the word *Messiah* we remind ourselves of Jesus' Jewish heritage and His fulfillment of the call.

earth? The one who went down is the same one who went
up above all the heavens so that he could fulfill all things.
(Ephesians 4:7-10)

There is a textual problem here. When we read the words *it
says* in our New Testament, we tend to think we are going to get a
quote from the Old Testament. The quote that Paul provides
above is certainly related to Psalm 68:18, but if you have a look in
your Bible you will see that Ps 68:18 states that God *"received* gifts
among men." *Received,* as opposed to what Paul says—*gave.* And
of course the word *gave* is important for Paul's point about God
giving gifts to the church. Did Paul quote his Bible incorrectly?![27]

Psalm 68 was probably used in ancient times to celebrate a
victory in battle. It was a common occurrence back then that a
king or general might go out with his army to fight a battle. If he
conquered his enemy, he would return to his homeland in a sort of
triumphal parade, with the heroic soldiers marching proudly into
town, bearing gifts from the plunder that they had taken. At the
end of the parade were the prisoners of war who were sentenced to
death, presented to the people as a spectacle of shame. [28]

In the past I had applied this metaphor of the triumphal return
to Ephesians 4, and ignored Paul's use of a different word when
quoting the psalm.[29] But, knowing that Paul is a wordsmith,

---

[27] Remember that the only Bible Paul had was the Hebrew scriptures, the
collection of Jewish documents that Christians now call the Old Testament.
Like most early Christians, Paul probably used the Septuagint, the Greek
translation of the Hebrew Bible, though his training would have given him
access to the Hebrew scrolls as well.

[28] For example, see Col 2:15, and I Cor 4:9 where Paul uses this same triumphal
return metaphor to compare the ministry of the apostle to being a prisoner at
the end of the parade!

[29] It certainly can be seen to make sense—the leadership gifts listed in verse 11
could be plunder from the battle against satan.

deliberate about the way he says things, I felt unsatisfied with this avoidance. Then one day I learned more about this passage from an expert on Ephesians, Thorsten Moritz.[30]

What we find out from Professor Moritz is that over time Psalm 68 came to be used in the celebration of the Day of Pentecost, which was originally a harvest festival, but was turned into a celebration of the giving of the Law after the Jews returned from the exile. Since that was about God *giving* something (the Law, or Torah), the Jews switched the wording for the sake of the celebration.

Because Paul intends to talk about Jesus giving leaders as gifts to the church, he decides to make use of this more recent Jewish pattern of using Ps 68:18 to celebrate the giving of the Torah from the top of the mountain. (Moses went up to receive it, and came down from the heights bearing God's great gift.) But now Paul raises things to a whole new level.

He takes the pattern that is common in the Jewish usage of his time, and applies it to the greatest gift God ever gave—not the Torah, but the Messiah. And then he turns it around and says, not only is Messiah the gift of God, but Messiah is the incarnate God who came down to the lowest parts of the earth and then ascended above the heavens so that He could shower grace gifts upon His people.

What grace gifts did Messiah give?

---

[30] Sometimes we need to go to the experts. Exegetes and theologians also are a gift to the church, to help us understand our Bibles more correctly. Thorsten Moritz is Professor of New Testament at Bethel Seminary in St Paul, Minnesota. He knows more about the letter to the Ephesians than I do, so he helped me untangle this problem. But you can also consult the experts by checking a particular verse in a good commentary. For assistance in choosing a good commentary, see the helpful index in *How to Read the Bible* by Fee & Stuart, which is listed in the bibliography.

And he himself gave not only apostles, but also prophets and evangelists and pastors and teachers. Why? For the preparation of the saints for the work of ministry, so that the body of Messiah would be built up until we all arrive at the unity of the faith and of the knowledge of the Son of God. When this happens, the body of Messiah (the church) will be like a full-grown man, having achieved the measure of the stature of the fullness of Messiah.

Then we will no longer be babies, wave-tossed and blown about by every wind-blast of teaching, easily influenced by the cunningness of people, by craftiness and deceitful methods.

But rather, living with integrity, in love, we the body are expected to grow up in every way until we fit to the head, who is Messiah. How can this happen? Well, because the whole body is joined together and held together by him, making use of every supporting ligament in a way that is appropriate to the function of each part. This brings about the growth of the body as it builds itself up in love. (Ephesians 4:11-16)

The grace gifts that Messiah gives in this example are all leadership gifts.[31]

Now let's practice what we've learned about lists. Remember, Paul's lists are *ad hoc*. That means that we ought not to think that these five[32] leadership gifts are the only five that the church needs, or that all five have to be present in every church gathering. Indeed, Paul himself lists other leadership gifts throughout his

---

[31] Notice that this is not the typical mixed list of charismata, but a pure one— of leadership gifts this time.

[32] Some people would say four because teacher and pastor seem to be linked by the way they are listed in the Greek.

writings—deacon, elder, and overseer, for example. No, these are the five that Paul particularly thought of when he wrote this letter to Christians in Asia Minor in the second half of the first century.[33] He chooses these leadership gifts because they are good examples for making his point.

And what is Paul's point? Read the passage again. Jesus, the great gift of God, distributes gifts to His church. These gifts are various kinds of leaders, and the leaders are given a significant task. According to Paul, the reason Messiah gives leaders to the church is that they are to *prepare the saints for the work of ministry.* In other words, the leaders are portrayed by Paul as being rather like *trainers* who coach and encourage and pass on skills to all the people in the church so that the people can do the ministry.

> Dan: "As a future youth leader, my job is to train and teach teens to do ministry—not just come up with a funny message or cool music for entertainment."

Now, is this how we usually function in the church today? Do we meet Sunday mornings (or whenever) for hands-on "training sessions" so that the people of God can be more effective in their ministries? I'm sad to say that many churches tend to think something like this: The church has hired the pastor and the pastoral staff, and since we are paying them wages, they are the ones who ought to do "the work of the ministry." The pastor(s) should preach and organize and counsel and keep the youth out of

---

[33] If you look at the footnotes in your Bible at the beginning of Ephesians, you will discover that the earliest surviving manuscripts of this letter do not have "to the Ephesians" as the address. Many scholars therefore believe that this letter was meant as an encyclical, to be passed around to a number of churches (see Col 4:16 for evidence that Paul did this with his letters), and that Ephesus was perhaps the main city that preserved and reproduced the letter. This more general audience would also explain why Ephesians is one of Paul's two most formal letters. He didn't have a specific local church in mind, but rather was writing a letter that would be meaningful for various churches in an area.

trouble and visit the sick and represent the church in the community and administrate the finances, and so forth.

Reflect: Is this how you have been taught to see your church leadership? What might be some dangers inherent in this understanding?

But what is Paul teaching us here? The leaders are given as gifts to the church to train and equip the saints—that's all us regular folks—so that *we* can use *our* gifts to do the ministry. Sunday morning gatherings of the church should not be set up as programs, or shows, where we come to watch the leaders perform (and then we critique them), but rather as an ongoing education, including not only the teaching of healthy theology but also the passing on of life skills, ministry skills, etc.

And most of these skills are best taught not by the lecture method but by interactive practical strategies.

Let's take one example. We have all sat and chafed under high-power preaching about how we ought to be evangelizing—telling everyone about Jesus and helping them to surrender to Him as Lord and Savior of their lives. And we all agree with those sermons—they are, after all, true—and we feel guilty that we haven't lived up to the command of God to go out and convert the world.

What is the problem? It is not that the saints lack information or love for the lost, or even that they lack dedication. But they do lack not only skills, but even the necessary *framework* for evangelism.

> John: "I'm usually the one "yelling at" the people to get up and do God's work."

The leaders are not equipping the saints, they are yelling at them—no matter how gently. *Telling* the people to do something is not at all the same as equipping them—helping them become able and willing to do it.

What would be a better solution?

First of all, we need to look around and recognize that there are people in the church who are grace gifts from Jesus in the area of evangelism. They are called to this vital task and they enjoy it immensely. This is a combination of personality (they *like* to talk to strangers), and calling (it burns within them to tell everyone about Jesus).

So does that mean that the rest of us are off the hook? No, but it does mean that we don't need to fill the shoes of those called to the task of evangelism as leaders. Far more, it means that our evangelistically gifted leaders ought to be strategizing about ways to help all God's people bring their friends to Jesus.

> Phil: *"When my heart soaks in the love of God for me, I see others without this great gift and I long for them to experience it also."*

Obviously, the methods of the called and gifted evangelist don't often work for regular folks. We may be shy, unskilled at persuasion, embarrassed, afraid of rejection. Our hearts are in the right place, but we are trembling in our boots. Maybe we will go out and do contact evangelism once or twice out of a sense of duty, but we will not continue in it as a lifestyle because it costs us so much emotionally.

Reflect: Has this been your experience with evangelism? Tell some stories.

So what should our leaders do? We've already agreed that preaching another sermon on evangelism is not the answer. We also agree that it isn't God's plan for us to expect the gifted evangelists to do all the evangelism. Far from it!

Dear pastor, please train us, teach us, encourage us. Make use of the weekly large church gathering[34] as a coaching session to equip us to help our friends find Jesus. People do have grace gifts that will be great tools in drawing others to God, but they are not usually the same grace gifts that the called evangelist has. Not everyone in the church is able to persuade people with words, but everyone can be used in concert to draw people to the kingdom.

If you were hoping for a practical strategy for evangelism at this point, hold on. I'm going to come back to it.

Results of equipping the saints

In Ephesians 4, Paul goes on to detail the resulting character-istics of a church in which the leaders equip the people to do the ministry. He says that such a church is "expected to grow up in every way until we fit with the head, who is Messiah." It's really a funny picture when you think about it. Here is Jesus the Messiah, who is the fully mature head. And attached to this adult head is a baby body. The reason that Jesus puts leaders in the church is to encourage and enable that baby body to "grow up" and become an adult body so that the body matches its head in stature, or maturity.

Out-workings of this increasing maturity are then listed by Paul: unity, healthier theology, maturity of the individuals,

---

[34] You will notice that I focus on the main Sunday morning gathering as the place to equip the saints. Why not at the Wednesday night prayer meeting or during Sunday school? If your church has 80% or better attendance at other weekly meetings, fine, use those meetings for some of these things. But most churches only bring the whole body of Christ together once a week. If something is important enough to do at all, it is important enough to do it with everyone. This requires a re-thinking of what ought to happen on Sunday (or whenever your main gathering is). We will continue to flesh this out in the following chapters.

stability, resistance to heresy, effectiveness in ministry, and love for each other. That's what an adult body would look like as it begins to fit to its head—Jesus.

In a church that is taking seriously the call to equip the saints, we would also expect to find that many of the regular folks are gaining skills in various leadership giftings, learning to preach and teach, to guide the body into worship, to mentor and disciple others, to receive vision from God for the body and to develop strategies to achieve that vision.

How would this equipping for leadership look in practice? Well, if a pastoral leader suspects that a church member has the gift to preach, for example, the pastor might strategize ways to help this person test and grow into their gift. The person could be asked to give a devotional or mini-sermon some Sunday, guided by the leadership in preparation, and given feedback afterward. As the person gains confidence and skills, s/he can be allowed to preach longer sermons, still with feedback. In time, those who are gifted for preaching might become part of the leadership team, a group of gifted communicators to draw from according to the guidance of the Holy Spirit as the church pursues God together.

I have been sad to witness a different scenario. Often, a pastor will give a responsibility to a church member, perhaps to preach or to lead worship. That person is thrown into the job with no guidance or training and expected to know what to do. Occasionally, a mature person will be able to step into a new responsibility without help and will do a great job at it. But even then, a distance has been created between pastor and member, so that there is no expectation of accountability or teamwork in future planning. You may end up with a worship leader who creates his/her own little kingdom and refuses to submit to the direction of the church as a whole. More often, a person thrown into leadership will not do well, receive no feedback, and never be asked to do this ministry again, creating hurt feelings, resentment, and resistance to future ideas presented by the leadership.

In order to avoid such unhappy scenarios, church leaders often fail to equip people for ministry at all, thinking that is a simpler and safer approach. Take no risks, clean up no messes.

But it is actually quite dangerous to avoid the pitfalls by keeping people sitting in the pews. When the saints are not equipped for ministry by their leaders, what do they do? They might just stay babies, needing to be fed, pampered, and diapered for the rest of their lives. Far too many Christians have never been discipled, held accountable, encouraged to find God's call on their life, and released into effective ministry.

This lack of discipleship is one reason why American Christians are often apathetic, materialistic, and ineffective in impacting our culture. It may also be why increasing numbers of Christians no longer come to weekly church gatherings—they see no reason for passive attendance at a program that is not impacting their lives.

On the other hand, unequipped Christians might be so hungry for spiritual growth that they will go looking for adult food elsewhere. At best this is likely to damage the unity and stability of the local body, but at worst it can result in undiscerning (because immature) believers who accept outside teachings

> Danielle: "This is the case at the universities—activism apart from Jesus arises out of a desire to shape and change the world. Students have no outlet in the church."

that are unhealthy, unbalanced, or even heretical. If healthy leaders don't equip the saints, the saints become vulnerable to every wind of doctrine or unexamined experience that blows their way.

Reflect: Have you witnessed any of these results of not discipling the saints? Has someone invested in your life, helping you to become all God intended? If so, share examples from that process.

An example of a charismatic strategy for liberating the laity

You probably already realize that liberating the laity (or equipping the saints) and having a charismatic understanding of the church fit together like a hand in a glove. Let's take a closer look, coming back to that need for better strategy for evangelism that we discussed earlier.

The Alpha Course is an excellent example of a charismatic strategy for evangelism. While I was at St Stephen's Church in Birmingham, England, for three wonderful years, they instituted the Alpha Course as part of their evangelistic strategy. I was privileged to witness how this beautifully gift-based strategy involved the whole church in drawing people to God.

Those who were gifted in leadership and organizational skills carefully planned and implemented a period of preparation and teaching, so that when the course started nearly all the members of the church were emotionally invested and practically involved. The leaders trained the people for ministry and helped them find a place where they could be effective.

There were many people who sent out invitations and/or brought their friends to the course.[35] Others who were gifted and called to prayer invested much time praying and fasting for people

---

[35] Members were encouraged to join their friends as participants. Notice that this would place the member strategically (and truthfully) as a friend and fellow learner. As a result, if questions should arise in the future, the guest will naturally turn to the friend who invited him/her and start a conversation, removing the need for the church member to initiate some sort of "presentation" of the gospel.

to come to Alpha. When the Alpha Course began, there were gifted men and women who cooked, set, and served a lovely meal. Still others prepared and presented a short provocative teaching, using the simple guidelines and materials provided by Alpha.

After the meal and the teaching, the participants split into smaller groups, consisting of one or two discussion leaders (mature church members who had been trained by the organizational leaders), several other Christians, and their invited friends who wanted to know more about Christianity. The leaders led a discussion time in which everyone was encouraged to share and no one was allowed to dominate. The Christians who participated in the groups had been taught to avoid being know-it-alls who always had the right answer, but rather to treat the opinions of the seekers with respect even though they may have seemed off-base or naïve. Meanwhile another group of Christians was washing dishes in the kitchen.

Everyone had a part to play in drawing people into the kingdom of God. Some were gifted in people-skills or communication. Others were gifted in hospitality skills such as cooking or decorating or cleaning. Without that lovely meal, the whole Alpha concept

> John: "Grasping this concept can help us fight the desire to rise above our co-laborers in Christ and remain humble servants."

falls apart. It is dependent on those who are able to create an atmosphere of welcome. And you may be aware that the Alpha Course has been singularly effective in helping people find their way to God. It is a great example both of what it means for a church to be truly charismatic, and of how everyone in a church can be involved in evangelism—and be happy about it!

So, instead of preaching yet another sermon on how we ought to be saving the lost, this church strategized, looked at giftings, and taught skills, thus helping all the people to be involved in reaching out to those who do not yet know God. And notice one more thing—because the people developed their giftings and learned new skills, they are able to continue to use these whether the church does the Alpha course again or not. As a result, the St Stephens church body grew up a little bit more into Messiah, who is its head.

Reflect: Has your church or group used a similar strategy that made use of many different giftings among God's people to achieve a common goal? Talk about what worked and what needed further strategic development.

The Priesthood of All Believers

The priesthood of the believer is a concept that can be found throughout the NT in more subtle expressions, and you should watch for it as you read. But there are a few passages that refer to it directly.

> And you, like living stones, are built into a spiritual house, as a holy priesthood, to bring spiritual sacrifices that are pleasing to God through Jesus Christ. For it says in the scripture…"You are a chosen race, a royal priesthood, a holy nation, a people belonging (to God), so that you might proclaim the excellencies of the one who called you out of darkness into his marvelous light. Those who were formerly not a people are now the people of God.
> (Excerpts from I Peter 2:5-10—see the whole context)

> To the one who loves us and released us from our sins by his blood, and made us a kingdom, priests to his God and father, to him be glory and might for ever and ever, amen.
> (Revelation 1:5b-6)

Both of these passages are concerned to show that the new people of God who came into existence on the Day of Pentecost, are a fulfillment of the ancient Jewish understanding that they (the Jews) were themselves a kingdom of priests and a holy chosen nation.[36] Here are a few of the many passages from the Hebrew Bible that gave the Jews this identity and presaged the identity of the followers of Jesus, their Messiah.

> Now then, if you will indeed obey My voice and keep My covenant, then you shall be My own possession among all the peoples, for all the earth is Mine; and you shall be to Me a kingdom of priests and a holy nation.
> (Exodus19: 5-6a)

> But you will be called the priests of the Lord; You will be spoken of as ministers of our God.
> (Isaiah 61:6)

What exactly is a priest?

Various Christian traditions have developed the idea of priesthood to fit their context. Some more liturgical groups like the Orthodox, Catholic, or Anglican churches have maintained the priesthood as something separate from the position of the ordinary believer. Only some people are anointed as priests, and the priests perform duties in the gathering of believers that others are not allowed to do. Priests are often seen as having special access to God.

The evangelical type churches have a tendency to give lip service to the priesthood of all believers, but they still often separate the pastor out as the only person who is allowed to

---

[36] You may already be aware that *holy* does not mean particularly good. It means *set apart*. The people of God, whether under the old or the new covenant, are holy, not because of any actions of their own, but because God has chosen them to be His people.

preach, marry, bury, serve communion, or perform other ministries. When they teach on the priesthood of all believers, they tend to refer to the congregation fulfilling its priestly calling in worship or prayer.

There are egalitarian traditions as well, such as the Quakers, where all of the members of a local church are potentially able to take part in all forms of ministry, according to calling, maturity, and willingness.[37] These traditions come closest to achieving a sense of being a kingdom of priests. But even here we see a tendency to think that the priestly duties involve mostly the visible leadership activities.

The most helpful illustration of priesthood that I have heard is that of a *bridge-builder*. A priest is someone who builds a bridge between people and God, who brings them together. If we now combine this with our understanding of what it means to be charismatic, it will fit beautifully. The charismata are all ways of building bridges between people and God, and drawing them together.

One person's gift of fervent prayer will bring his/her friend before the throne of God as s/he intercedes for the friend's health. Another's gift of a word of knowledge will help the whole church understand the heart of God for a situation in their neighborhood. Someone else may have

> Jim: "This needs to be taught and explained more in our churches."

gifts of hospitality and kindness that demonstrate the love and acceptance that God has for a stranger newly arrived in our midst. And of course, the leadership gifts also are to be used to draw people to God through healthy teaching, singing worship songs, organizational skills, and so on.

------

[37] My Quaker grandmother conducted many a funeral.

Reflect: In what ways does God use you as a priest who draws people close to God?

If our priestly ministry is based on our gifting, we may find that the typical expectations of who does what in the church will receive a shaking up. You may have a pastor in your church who is gifted at counseling, but only a fair public speaker. Typically this would lead to a pastor under pressure to perform in an area of his/her weakness, and a dissatisfied church. Wouldn't it be so much more pleasing to God if we could release the pastor to excel in his/her priestly strengths, and look for other leadership-quality people in the church to take on the priestly ministry of teaching or preaching?

If I am actively engaged in using my grace gifts to draw people closer to God and/or to represent people before God, I am exercising my priestly ministry.

The Church 4 as Family

Here is one final over-arching principle that we need to understand from the New Testament. The scriptural language of church as family is often overlooked because it is so integrated into the Bible. It is assumed by the authors of scripture, rather than taught. Watch for family language (brothers, sisters, mothers, fathers, households) as you read your New Testament. Jesus, Paul, and John in particular simply assume an attitude that comes naturally to them because of one of the strengths of their culture. Middle Eastern cultures were (and still are today) *collective* cultures. Western individualism would be a foreign concept to them. It would never occur to them to say, "I can worship God better by myself out in the woods," or "I don't need to go to church to be a Christian." And Middle Eastern gatherings would be more welcoming and family-like than the typical Western church.

Ashok: "An Indian student I led to Christ asked me, 'Why should I come to church? I feel more lonely in church than among my Hindu friends.'"

Immediately following the outpouring of the Spirit on the Day of Pentecost we see that the new believers intuitively gathered into family-like groups. They met together in the temple, but also in homes. They shared meals together. Throughout Acts and the Epistles we get the sense that churches are often based in homes, that the heads of households often become the church leaders, and that those who join them, though not biologically related, are treated as one of the family.

How should Western churches respond to the recognition that the first-century church was much more family-like than most of us currently are? Some groups try to force first-century Middle Eastern culture on Americans, as if it were somehow ordained by God. That is surely not the answer.

Instead we need to look for natural gathering points in our culture, both as an expression of who we are in Jesus, and in order to be able to tap into existing structures. When I was a campus missionary in Koeln,[38] Germany, I found myself in a culture that is at least as individualistic as America. It became clear that if we wanted to build something like family among university students, our strategy would have to be deliberate and determined. Because eating together is one of the most effective ways to build relationships, we began to meet once and then twice a week at the student cafeteria for lunch. As pastor, I arrived early and stayed late so there would always be at least me sitting at our regular table when someone would come by to look for us.

Some days two or three people would eat together. Some days we would fill several tables.[39] We might have deep theological discussions, passionate arguments, or become hilariously silly. One person might bring a non-Christian friend and introduce him/her to the group. They would all welcome this new friend

---

[38] You may know this city as Cologne.

[39] Notice you need a strategy for when another person arrives at an already full table. Someone from the leadership team needs to be ready to move to a new table, perhaps taking several others with him/her, and making the newcomer feel honored rather than an interruption.

into the "family" and take on corporate responsibility for showing God's love to him/her. In fact, a number of non-Christians became regulars at the "Stammtisch," and then came to our worship gatherings or retreats and found faith in Jesus.

My calling in Koeln was to reach university students, but I noticed a cultural opening among native Koelners that I hope someone will plug into some day. I learned that there are very few Koeln natives (whose family roots go back many generations in the city) in the evangelical or pentecostal churches. It seemed nearly impossible to reach this people group with the gospel. However, a large percentage of Koelner have a habit of spending several evenings each week in the nearest *Kneiper*. A Kneiper would be a small pub located within two or three blocks of their home. The same people go there all the time, and yes, they have a beer, but what they are looking for and finding is family-like relationships with their neighbors. They may have been going there for 10, 20, 30 years. Perhaps their parents went there before them.

Now, my idea would not be the sort of outreach that could be successful in a few months or even a few years. It might take a year or more just to be accepted as part of the regulars. But I could imagine a weekly Bible study that meets in the home of one of the believers. Instead of serving a dessert in the hidden safety of the host apartment, what if the whole group made a habit of ending their time together by going together to the nearest Kneiper. At first they would simply sit at their table and enjoy each other's company. But over time, the regulars would begin to become curious and talk about this visiting group. Eventually someone would break the ice and begin to talk across cultural lines. And, if they persevere, this group of Christians could experience two wonderful things—being accepted as guests and finally being invited as adopted family into the native culture, as well as being able to minister to people who would otherwise be unreachable.

Reflect: Have you noticed any natural gathering points in your neighborhood? Do you see possible ways to express what it means to be the family of God in American culture?

The weekly family reunion

This paradigm is not perfect, but I'd like to encourage you to begin thinking and speaking of your regular gatherings—particularly Sunday mornings—in the language of *family reunion.* This will help to redirect people's expectations of what should happen when you come together. Hopefully they will begin to understand that it is not about putting on a program but about getting together with people who have become precious to us and who have a common goal of being God's people together. We will refer back to this idea in the following chapters.

What we have learned about being God's people

If we take everything discussed so far, we can draw the following conclusions.

- God still speaks to His people today.
- God's people are like a family—they love each other and like to hang out. They treat newcomers like family as well.
- All God's people have gifts to share when they come together.
- Some of the gifts that God gives are manifestation gifts—supernatural abilities that reveal God in the midst of His people.
- When God's people gather, they should be expecting God to interact with them in some way, perhaps through the manifestation gifts.
- God's people should use all of their great variety of gifts to build up the whole body of believers.

- When they do that, they build bridges between God and people, which is their priestly ministry.

Based on this list, as well as other principles you have learned along the way, we should be starting to recognize that there are some important things missing from many church gatherings. It is not about worship style or order of service or personal preferences. The principles we are learning here can be present or absent in any type of church gathering, no matter what the denomination. Let's see what we can learn from the New Testament about church gatherings, and then talk about practical ways to begin to grow and mature.

The New Testament Pattern for the Gathering of Believers

Here is an overview of key New Testament passages for the gathered church.

On whom does the Spirit fall?

Acts 2 tells us about a gathering of believers that straddles the era of the Old Covenant and the era of the New Covenant. Jesus' followers had spent time with Him after the resurrection, and then they watched Him ascend into heaven after He had explained to them that they were going to receive some sort of power. They did the "pentecostal" thing of waiting and expecting, and then it happened. Maybe we should read it again:

> When the time arrived for the Day of Pentecost, they were all together in the same place. Suddenly a roar came out of heaven. It was like a violent driving wind and it filled the whole house where they were sitting. What appeared

> to them then were tongues, as if of fire, being distributed,
> and they rested upon each one of them. They were all
> filled with the Holy Spirit and began to speak in other
> languages, as the Spirit gave them ability to speak.
> (Acts 2:1-4)

Remember that we pointed out that the Spirit fell on *everyone*, not just on the leaders, and that this is likely what caused Peter to realize that he was witnessing the fulfillment of the prophecy of Joel. Notice also that the experience was physical, and that it was sudden and unexpected.

They all rushed out into the streets, praising God and continuing to speak in these (to them) unknown languages. This drew a crowd, and Peter preached his great Pentecost sermon, explaining the good news to Jewish pilgrims who were already primed to respond, and 3000 people became part of the new people of God on that first day.

What is the natural response?

This new people of God immediately began to sense a common identity, and they expressed it in large part by *gathering together*. The experience of Pentecost gave them such a sense of belonging to each other that they acted like families—eating together, sharing possessions, hanging out. Notice that they met in smaller groups (in homes) and in larger groups (in the temple).

> As often as possible, they sought out chances to gather, to
> hear the teaching of the apostles, to eat together, and to
> pray. Everyone felt a kind of tingling fear, and there were
> all sorts of miracles and signs happening through the
> apostles. All the believers stayed together in one place,
> and they shared everything. They started selling their
> property and possessions so they could share with those
> who didn't have anything. Every day they sought to be

together in the temple, as well as eating together in the houses, sharing in the food with gladness and sincere hearts, praising God and enjoying the favor of all the people. And every day the Lord added people who were being saved to their gatherings.
(Acts 2:42-47)

Reflect: What principles can you find in this passage concerning what it means to be the people of God? Brainstorm together about ways that your church could live out these principles in your context.

The body as metaphor for the church

Romans 12:3-8 is one of several places where Paul uses the picture of the human body, and the need for every part of the body to be active in order to have healthy function.

For I speak by the grace given me to everyone among you—to each of you according to the measure of faith that God has given you: Do not think more highly of yourself than you ought, but think sensibly. For just as we have many body parts in one body, and the parts do not all have the same function, so also we the many are one body in Messiah, and parts of each other. We have different grace gifts based on the grace given to us. Let's use them well. If your grace gift is prophecy, then use it as much as you have faith. The same way with grace gifts like serving others, teaching, or encouraging. If your grace gift is donating, then be liberal. If it is management, do it diligently. If it is acts of mercy, do them cheerfully.
(Romans 12:3-8)

The human body is a particularly apt metaphor for the church. A body is a living organism, composed of many separate parts that cannot even live, let alone function, apart from each other. Yet every part has significance, even if it is hidden, or embarrassing.

Paul expands on this idea in I Cor 12. We've quoted excerpts of it earlier, but let's read the whole section through this time.

> John: "If every part is not active, we will miss some of what God is saying to us."

There are distributions of grace gifts, but the one Spirit, and there are distributions of ministries, but the one Lord, and there are distributions of workings, but the one God, who works all things in all people.

But to each person is given the manifestation of the Spirit for the benefit of all. To one person is given a word of wisdom by means of the Spirit. To another is given a word of knowledge according to the same Spirit. To another faith by the same Spirit, to another grace gifts of healings in the one Spirit, to another workings of miracles, to another prophecy, to another the ability to discriminate between spirits, to another varieties of tongues, to another the ability to interpret tongues.

But all things are worked by one and the same Spirit, who distributes to each person as He sees fit.

For just as the body is one entity with many parts—and even though there are many parts in a body it is still one body—so it is with the Messiah. For we were all baptized in one Spirit into one body, whether we are Jews, Gentiles, slaves, or free, and we were all made to drink the one Spirit.

For the body is not just one part, but many parts. If the foot should say, "I am not a hand, so I am not part of the body," would this statement make it not part of the body? And if the ear should say, "I am not an eye, so I am not part of the body," would this make it not part of the body?

If the whole body were an eye, how would it hear?! If the whole body were an ear, how would it smell?!

So this is the deal: God has placed the parts—each one of them—in the human body just as He wished. If they were all the same part, where would the body be? But the reality is that there are many parts and one body. The eye cannot say to the hand, "I don't need you," nor the head to the feet, "I don't need you." On the contrary, the parts of the body that seem to be the weakest are the most necessary ones. And the parts of the body that seem embarrassing to us? These we surround with greater honor. And we cover our unpresentable parts with greater modesty. Of course the presentable parts don't need to be covered.

That's how God created the human body—giving greater honor to the lesser part—so that there might not be division in the body, but that the parts might care the same for each other. If one part suffers, all the parts suffer together. If one part is honored, all the parts rejoice together.

The church is just like this illustration of the human body—you all are the body of Messiah and individually parts of each other. God placed the following people in the church: first apostles, second prophets, third teachers, then miraculous acts of power, then grace gifts of healings, helpers, leadership abilities, and kinds of tongues. Are all of you apostles? Do you all prophesy? Do you all teach? Do all of you work miracles? Do all of you have grace gifts of healings? Do all of you bring messages in unknown languages? Do all of you interpret messages in unknown languages? Of course not.
(I Corinthians 12:4-28)

So that list of the manifestations of the Spirit in verses 7-11 is to be understood in the context of the body. It is interwoven into the whole idea of the church being like a human body with many parts. Just as our eyes and feet and nose are all necessary for the full functioning of our physical bodies, so the manifestation gifts—and indeed all the grace gifts—are needed for the church to be fully functioning.

Why do we share our gifts? The next section of Paul's letter to the Corinthians tells us that the only legitimate reason to share our gifts is because we love each other.

You will remember our discussion earlier in the book, that I Corinthians 13 demonstrates that love is not the highest gift but rather the framework for all the gifts. If we share grace gifts for reasons of pride or to get attention or to gain power over others, those gifts are like someone banging pots and pans together—just noise and distraction.

Reflect: Talk about how Paul's teaching about the embarrassing and unpresentable parts of the body can be applied in your church or group.

How to have an orderly church

Chapter 14 of I Corinthians takes the foundation that Paul has built in the previous two sections and applies it to some specific problems the Corinthians are having. What we surmise about them from chapters 12-14 is that they have come to imagine that speaking in "tongues of men and of angels" is proof of having attained some sort of spiritual elite status.[40] As a result, they wish

---

[40] In fact, many scholars think that their pagan, early gnostic, background has caused them to develop a theology of the resurrection of the spirit only, seeing tongues as a proof that they have already been united with God in the heavenly realms. Their bodies, being evil, are to be left behind some day and therefore unimportant. This would explain why Paul has to spend chapter 15

to demonstrate their status, and their gatherings are characterized by a whole lot of chaotic shouting in unknown languages. They are not using their unknown languages to pray or worship in unity, and they are not giving messages in tongues with interpretation following. Rather, they are all speaking at the same time and without purpose.

Paul says no, *everything should be done in order.* The principle of order in the church tends to be misunderstood—and therefore misapplied—in our contemporary situations. So let's spend some time thinking it through.

In American churches, it is no longer likely that a majority of church members would be former gnostic pagans who would misunderstand the resurrection (see footnote), and speak in tongues without purpose when they gather. You might find a few strange gatherings where something like that happens, I suppose. But American gatherings are more likely to be tainted by lack of belief in the supernatural, leading to a failure to submit to the Holy Spirit in His intention to reveal Jesus to us. As with the Corinthians, the body is not listening to the head, but the disorder is of a different sort.

What might American disorder look like? If the body of believers has gathered to seek and honor God, and the Holy Spirit reveals in our midst that God would like us to sit in reverent silence, but the band keeps playing through the program they had planned, that would be disorder. If the Spirit reveals that God is manifesting His majesty in our midst, and that the proper response would be to fall on our faces before Him, but we continue to sit in our pews with our hands folded primly in front of us, we are out of

---

proving to them that their bodies *are* eternal and most certainly will be resurrected.

order. If the Spirit fills us with joy and says, "Get up and dance before the Lord!" but we remain seated, that is disorder.

Disorder is basically disobedience. Churches can learn to listen to and obey the Spirit, but many pastors and their parishioners are leery of "letting the Spirit loose." So, instead of yielding authority to the Holy Spirit (and giving up our own human control), we often express a sort of quiet disobedience.

When God calls for quiet, we should be quiet. When God calls for happy chaos, we should embrace it with abandon.

So What Did It Look Like When the Early Church Gathered?

In I Cor 14, Paul spends a lot of time demonstrating that speaking in unknown languages is not the only manifestation of the Spirit, and he urges believers to seek a diversity of revelatory gifts. Then he seems to realize that this particular group of believers really doesn't get what a gathering is supposed to be like. This is embarrassing for the Corinthians, but helpful for us, because their lack of understanding causes Paul to *describe a worship gathering*. What a valuable window into the first-century church, into what Paul considered to be the norm.

> How should it be then, brothers and sisters? It should be
> like this: When you come together, each of you has
> something. Here are examples: A psalm, a teaching, a
> revelation, a message in an unknown language, an
> interpretation of that message. Everything that happens
> should be for the building up of the whole body.
> (I Corinthians 14:26)

Think about how marvelously this short description of a first-century gathering of Christians meshes with what we have learned about the priesthood of all believers, the church as family, the charismata, and the body.

Reflect: Have each person in your small group take one aspect of what it means to be church (priesthood, family, body, giftedness, pentecostal, etc.), and briefly demonstrate how I Cor 14:26 fits with that aspect. What are some ways that your church or group could more closely follow the principles taught in this passage?

Unity with diversity

The passages we've just examined bring us to the principle of unity with diversity. Paul is determined that the believers understand that there are many gifts of a great variety, and that all of them are valuable. He never seeks *uniformity* among believers. Uniformity would expect everyone to act and look the same. Rather Paul emphasizes that the people should be in *unity*. Unity celebrates the differences without resulting in jealousy, power-plays, or other sinful attitudes that would divide the body.

The entire scripture supports unity with diversity, but let's end our overview of the New Testament pattern by looking at two passages that bring it out particularly well.

Remember our discussion of Ephesians 4? Let's review part of that passage.

> And he himself gave not only apostles, but also prophets and evangelists and pastors and teachers. Why? For the preparation of the saints for the work of ministry, so that the body of Messiah would be built up until we all arrive at the unity of the faith and of the knowledge of the Son of God. When this happens, the body of Messiah will be like a full-grown man, having achieved the measure of the stature of the fullness of Messiah.

> Then we will no longer be babies, wave-tossed and blown
> about by every wind-blast of teaching, easily influenced by
> the cunningness of people, by craftiness and deceitful
> methods.
>
> But rather, living with integrity, in love, we the body are
> expected to grow up in every way until we fit to the head,
> who is Messiah. How can this happen? Well, the whole
> body is joined together and held together by him, making
> use of every supporting ligament in a way that is
> appropriate to the function of each part. This brings about
> the growth of the body as it builds itself up in love.
> (Ephesians 4:11-16)

Notice that Jesus gives diverse leadership gifts to the church so that all the believers might be equipped for ministry and the body *might reach unity* which is described as a corporate connection to the Head, with each member doing his/her part, resulting in growth and the building up of the body in love. Notice how equipping leads to unity, which leads to maturity.

Reflect: Spend time together studying Eph 4:11-16. It is so packed with interconnected principles that you might want to draw a sort of outline to show how Paul develops his argument. If you have access to a white board or a chalkboard, that would help you to have a more visual way to work on it together.

Finally, turn to Paul's letter to the Colossians. The first 13 verses of chapter 3 are all about the sort of godly behavior that ought to characterize followers of Jesus. Verses 12 and 13 urge them to be "dressed in" humility, kindness, meekness, forgiveness, compassion—all traits that make unity possible. He then links this unity to the diversity of gifts that people bring to the gatherings.

Over all these things put on love, which is the bond that completes this unity. And let the peace of Messiah rule in your hearts. After all, you were called to this in one body. And become thanks-givers. Let the word of Messiah dwell in you all richly, in all wisdom, while you teach and admonish one another with psalms, hymns, and spiritual songs, singing with grace in your hearts to God. (Colossians 3:14-16)

> *Phil: "If we really love each other, we will honor the expression of Christ in each individual and embrace what the Holy Spirit is speaking through our brother or sister."*

Pray: As a group, pray through these verses, asking God to "dwell in you richly" as a family of believers who are seeking to live in love and unity.

The snapshot of the gathering of believers

Let's come back to that description of the gathering of believers in I Cor 14:26.

How should it be then, brothers and sisters? It should be like this: When you come together, each of you brings something to share. Here are examples: A psalm, a teaching, a revelation, a message in an unknown language, an interpretation of that message. Everything that happens in the gathering should be for the building up of the whole body.

I am really thankful that the Corinthian church was in such a theological and behavioral mess, because otherwise Paul might not have needed to provide them with this simple, straightforward description of what is normal, of what healthy gatherings of believers typically looked like in the first century. You can see clearly that the early church was "charismatic" in the sense we have been talking about. Everyone was expected to bring grace gifts to share, with the goal that the whole body would be built up.

What does this mean for us? Well, it certainly calls into question our tendency to have a few people up front sharing their same grace gifts (preaching and musicianship) every week while the rest of us sit and watch. According to Paul, room must be made for a variety of gifts and for active participation of all those who gather.

Don't worry. I'm not saying that people should sit in a circle every week and one after another share the gift they brought. Churches larger than 15 people would find this very cumbersome! But the principle is so important that we must search diligently for effective ways to make it a reality in our gatherings.

Let's see if we can find some ways to talk about the church that will help us climb out of the boxes we tend to live in.

How We "Do Church"

"If a person does not become what he understands, he does not really understand it."

Søren Kierkegaard

"To say and not to do is not to say."

Chinese proverb

Reflect: Re-read these two quotes and discuss why you think I included them here.

All of this exciting material about what it means to be part of God's church will not be of much value if it does not affect our behavior. Am I advocating another attempt to "return to the first-century church," or to find a new "law" of how believers ought to gather, with exacting rules and expectations? Far from it.

If we understand anything from the discussion we've already had, we understand that there is marvelous freedom and creativity in God's church. Rather than developing a new set of rules, each gathering of Christians is challenged to listen to the Holy Spirit and to obey Him as He guides them in their corporate faith journey.

The pastor holds the key

Back in my seminary days, I wrote a paper about my denomination, the Assemblies of God. One of the key books I read was a detailed study of the health of AG churches by a sociologist named Margaret Poloma. Perhaps the most important finding of Poloma's study is that senior pastors hold the key to the charismatic experience of their members, and that the charismatic experience of the church was directly related to church growth.[41]

Poloma pointed out (and I'm sure you can confirm this from your own experience) that it is in an accepting and encouraging atmosphere that the freedom to hear from and respond to God's Spirit becomes normal, and only the pastor has the influence necessary to enable such an atmosphere.

As part of her data-gathering, Poloma interviewed 246 pastors. One area of research that turned out to be significant in her study was what she termed the "Prophecy Scale." Pastors were rated by whether they had felt led by God to perform some specific act,

---

[41] Poloma did not mean to imply that large churches are better than smaller ones, nor that charismatic experience is directly related to growth in *non*-AG churches. Rather, the fact that the Assemblies of God claims to be pentecostal and charismatic appears to affect people's expectations, and they therefore base decisions about attending any particular AG church at least partially on whether that church is living up to its faith claims.

given a prophecy or an interpretation in a church gathering, heard God speak through a dream or vision, or given a prophecy privately to another person. She found that those pastors who scored high on this scale were much more likely to be serving churches of the highly charismatic or experiential type, and they were the most likely to be encouraging manifestations of the Spirit in the gatherings of believers. Though churches whose pastors encouraged religious experiences during worship were not always highly charismatic, "a high level of charismatic activities cannot be found where the pastors discourage them."[42]

If you are a pastor, the whole rest of this book is going to challenge (but hopefully also encourage) you to accept the responsibility for guiding your people into a closer corporate relationship with God. I'm going to try to provide you with tools, but this truly is a question of whether you actually believe that God still speaks in the midst of the gathering of His people. If you believe it, you will want to live it out.

If you are not a pastor, but a regular member of a congregation, let me exhort you to patience and understanding. Moving a group of people into deeper experience of God is not a simple matter. It takes both courage and skills, skills that are typically no longer taught in our Bible schools, seminaries, or other training opportunities for pastors. The best thing you can do for your pastor is to pray and encourage. When your pastor initiates new experiments in the church, support him/her and give gentle feedback, especially when something goes well.

-----

[42]pp. 77-87. Poloma added (pp. 89-90) that the normal Assembly of God is not a community formed around a strong prophetic or charismatic figure, but "around a minister who has personal experiences of charisma and who promotes the belief that such experiences are part of the normal Christian life....[I]t is the message rather than the leader that is 'prophetic.'"

Pray: Stop here and pray for your pastors. Make a commitment to continue to pray for them.

Pastors typically face two challenges. One is to bring a congregation to the point that they wish to experience this interactive relationship with God. The other challenge is a fear of "what might happen." Both of these challenges can be effectively met. The pastor will need to make use of healthy teaching, be willing to let it be a long process, be willing to experiment—and to have experiments fall flat—and be willing to correct people who go out of bounds. It can be much easier just to stick with same old same old.

How we "do church" teaches theology (and pneumatology and ecclesiology)

It pains me to observe how church leaders tend to put techniques and structures into place (or allow them to continue unquestioned) when these structures are in direct opposition to the theology the leaders claim to be convinced of. Many pastors who teach about the priesthood of all believers fail to train their people to do priestly ministry. Many would agree theoretically that the Holy Spirit gifts all people for ministry, but do not provide opportunities for those gifts to be practiced and developed. Pastors who tell their congregations that they are a family of believers expect them to sit in rows and passively watch a program on Sunday mornings. Is that how families behave when they gather?

What are we teaching our people about God and the world and salvation and mission if we treat them as an audience that watches a show every Sunday? What do we teach them about the community of believers if our worship music is so loud that people can't hear themselves singing, let alone be enriched by the passionate love for God expressed by the voice of their neighbor? What do we teach them about individual giftedness if we fail to recognize and appreciate their gifts in a public manner? What does it mean to equip the saints? Just to put them through a new members' class and then assign them to a committee? To convince them to show up at events the leaders have planned? That sounds more like using the saints than equipping them.

And of course, a large number of church members perpetuate this impoverished understanding of the church by expecting the pastor to do all the ministry—"It's what we pay him for!"

If we continue to follow established patterns without reflection

Heather: "It's sad that this happens. Every member of the church should visit the sick, etc."

on the message they send, then it won't matter how much lip service we give to being pentecostal or charismatic, or to supporting the priesthood of all believers. Our congregations will not believe in these principles if we are not doing them. If we want the saints to be equipped and the church to be healthy, we must all step back and re-consider how we "do church." What happens in our gatherings teaches what we really believe. It will either provide our people with healthy, Spirit-informed theology, or it will keep them immature and unmotivated.

> Directive leadership that defines truth, determines the mission, and decides the distribution of resources will of necessity create passive followership. Although an immature person needs this kind of leadership at the outset of his/her spiritual life, a wise leader will help his/her people begin to take responsibility, think biblically, understand and apply truth, envision the mission, and become engaged because it is "theirs." Leadership is not a static thing but must evolve with the maturity level of the congregation.
> Anita Koeshall

Reflect: See if you can come up with other examples of how our ways of "doing church" teach theology—whether healthy or not.

Knowing People,
Knowing God

At this point, I would like us to consider how people behave in interpersonal relationships—friends, families, married couples, relationships at work. (Don't worry, I haven't forgotten the topic of my book. This is going someplace.)

The first truth to affirm is that any healthy relationship should provide the people involved in it with security and a resting place, a place where the atmosphere is not one of ongoing anxiety, uncertainty, or fear. Stability is good. We need to be able to trust the people we spend most of our time with to be predictable and trustworthy.

However, we humans tend to take this need for security too far. We often place too much emphasis on establishing and maintaining a comfortable pattern, discouraging unexpected behavior, avoiding tension and conflict. We'd rather not be surprised. We certainly don't like to take risks. When this risk avoidance in human relationships and institutions becomes extreme, it might be described by such terms as *normalization* or *routinization*.

Normalization or routinization[43] would describe a relationship or social group where people have come to a point of no longer wishing or being able to change individually or to challenge the established ways of doing things. People fall into these unhealthy patterns because of a felt need for predictability. If you conform, you will not be noticed or challenged to grow and change.

But milquetoast predictability is not good for relationships! In friendships, marriages, families, and work teams, avoiding risk is a risky thing to do. I'm sure you can think of relationships around you that would be improved if one or more of the people involved would do something that breaks out of the ordinary, whether that might be learning to say "I'm sorry," refusing for once to be manipulated, bringing home roses, or trying creative ideas in an area of their common life that has become ho-hum. Same-old same-old often leads to complacency, boredom, even unfaithfulness.

In summary, a healthy relationship, while allowing us to feel safe, must also challenge us to go outside of our comfort zones and face pain, risk confrontation, accept the existence of discord, etc. Taking risks in relationships causes people to grow, to deepen and broaden, both personally and corporately.

Relationships are what the church is all about

As we've discussed in the previous chapters, Christians are in relationship to the other members of the body. Everything that

---

[43] In sociology, normalization is a process whereby artificial norms of behavior are made to seem natural and wanted, through influence, imitation, and conformity.

Routinization has more to do with making something into a habit or standard procedure. It is a set of customary and often mechanically performed procedures or activities we've just said about the need to have both stability and challenge in human relationships applies to the church. We will discuss these human to human relationships when we explore the idea of family reunion at the end of this chapter.

But there is another relationship. We have a relationship with God, both as individuals and corporately—as members of the larger community of believers. We can say much the same things about this relationship. Yes indeed, there is a safe place in God, a place where we are accepted and loved no matter what stupid and shameful things we have done, a place where we have a home, and where we do not need to be anxious or fearful.

> Kris: "If people feel secure, they will be more willing to face pain, confrontation, discord, etc."

But remember the insightful comment of Mr. Beaver in *The Lion, the Witch, and the Wardrobe*. Mr. Beaver explained to Lucy that the great lion, Aslan (who is an allegory for Jesus), is a good lion, but he is not a *tame* lion. God is good, but God is not tame. God is not entirely predictable nor at all controllable. Life with God will not be only sweet and lovely and cozy. It can be dangerous, scary, uncomfortable, or painful to be in the presence of God. According to the scripture, these aspects are a normal part of knowing God.[44]

> Ashok: "Twice I have seen God 'hit' people with his power sovereignly during worship. God chose to show these students (I interviewed them later) how BIG he was by simply overwhelming them by his powerful presence."

I could recount numerous times when I've felt God's presence during corporate worship not as joy or comfort (though that happens plenty often), but as a challenge to step into the unknown

---

[44] You may want to spend some time puzzling over scriptural examples of this God who is not tame. For a start, have a look at Exodus 4:21-26; Isaiah 5; Matthew 14:22-33; 16:21-23; Mark 9:14-29; and Acts 5:1-16.

or a rebuke for stubborn sin. Several times the Holy Spirit has put

> Aaron: *"The presence of an infinitely holy and just God should bring us to our knees."*

His finger on my deepest sorrow and invited me to embrace the pain in wrenching sobs. Thank God I've been surrounded by fellow believers who understood and supported what was happening, who were not confused or upset by it.

Reflect: Can you share similar instances of experiencing both the safety and the "danger" of God?

Are we avoiding God?

Now, let's think about how Christians tend to act when they gather together in God's presence. Leaders work hard to make the typical worship "service" in an American church feel safe, predictable, controllable, and comfortable. No matter if the music is lively or if people sing in tongues or go forward to an altar call. In most churches, the same things happen every Sunday morning, with little or

> Dan: *"We need to break out of our comfort zone, yet stay in tune with Christ."*

no variation. A plan has been made—an "order of service"—and the leaders lead the people through it. If a disturbance occurs, it makes everyone get a case of the fidgets. Why? Because the leaders and the congregation are treating the "service" like a performance, and performances are not to be interrupted or changed in mid-delivery.

Don't get me wrong—it is often exactly right that church gatherings would leave us feeling safe and secure. There are times when a person or the whole church just needs to be held close by God and reminded of God's unconditional love for us. But if our gatherings are only ever "nice," and pretty and pleasant, can we really say that we are experiencing the presence of God? Could it be that by avoiding risk and unpleasantness, we are also avoiding God?

Could it be that by avoiding risk, we are also avoiding God?

Reflect: Spend some time looking for other ways that relationship to people helps us understand relationship to God. Then come back to this question: How can we become healthier in all of our relationships? Are we avoiding each other? Are we avoiding God?

Worship is relationship with God

Worship, defined broadly here as what happens when God's people gather, is the most amazing thing. When we come together with each other, we also come together with God. For an hour or two, we make visible a relationship that eternally exists between the almighty God and the people of God. There is, or should be, a discernible interaction between the divine and the corrupt, between the infinite and the small.

How God longs to have a people who are in real relationship with Him, who seek to know Him, who listen and respond. All through the Hebrew scriptures—in the Law, the Prophets, and the Writings—the wistful longing expressed by Yahweh was for a people who would be His very own people from their whole hearts.

> The Lord will establish you as a holy people to Himself, as He swore to you, if you will keep the commandments of the Lord your God, and walk in His ways. So all the peoples of the earth shall see that you are called by the name of the Lord; and they shall be afraid of you. (Deuteronomy 28:9-10)

When You Come Together

Oh that My people would listen to Me. That Israel would walk in My ways! I would feed you with the finest of the wheat; and with honey from the rock I would satisfy you.
(Psalm 81:13, 16)

Like a shepherd He will tend His flock, in His arm He will gather the lambs, and carry them in His bosom; He will gently lead the nursing ewes.
(Isaiah 40:11)

I will pour out water on the thirsty land and streams on the dry ground; I will pour out My Spirit on your offspring, and My blessing on your descendants; and they will spring up among the grass like poplars by streams of water. This one will say, "I am the Lord's"; and that one will call on the name of Jacob; and another will write on his hand, "Belonging to the Lord," and will name Israel's name with honor.
(Isaiah 44:3-5)

My people have committed two evils: They have forsaken Me, the fountain of living waters, to hew for themselves cisterns, broken cisterns that can hold no water.
(Jeremiah 2:13)

I will put My law within them, and on their heart I will write it; and I will be their God, and they shall be My people. And they shall not teach again, each man his neighbor and each man his brother, saying, "Know the Lord," for they shall all know Me, from the least of them to the greatest of them," declares the Lord, "for I will forgive their iniquity, and their sin I will remember no more."
(Jeremiah 31:33-34)

I will give you a new heart and put a new spirit within you; and I will remove the heart of stone from your flesh and give you a heart of flesh. And I will put My Spirit within you and cause you to walk in My statutes and you

will be careful to observe My ordinances. And you will
live in the land that I gave to your forefathers; so you will
be My people, and I will be your God.
(Ezekiel 36:26-28)

And many more!

The New Testament records that there has been progress
toward the fulfillment of God's deep wish. Our corporate
relationship to God, already discernible in the OT, is described in
the New Testament with such pictures as a bride relating to the
groom, the physical body to the head, the family amongst its
members. (Notice how both Old and New Testament authors
provide us with examples from human relationships in order to
help us relate to God.)

Aids in building relationships

So what are the tools to healthy human relationships? You
know them: listening carefully, speaking honestly, giving and
receiving, sharing emotions, thoughts, decisions, etc, with the other
person. If you don't do these things in a human relationship, then
that relationship is immature or even unhealthy and dysfunctional.

It is the same with our relationship to God. There should be
real interaction, real back-and-forth sharing. If God's people meet
together, but do not interact with God, sharing emotions, thoughts,
and decisions, then the church is pursuing a dysfunctional and
unhealthy relationship with God.
On the other hand, mature

> John: "Many people don't know
> God like they should because we
> rarely allow God to speak to us."

corporate relationship to God will serve to reveal the presence of
God among us, and to strengthen the bond of love between God
and God's people.

Revelations that help us know God

Of course, there are aspects of our relationship to God that take us outside of our experience in human relationships. We worship God, but do not (ought not to) worship other people. God cannot normally be seen with our eyes, physically touched, audibly heard. God is unlimited and we are finite. We are not able to comprehend the mind of God except in small portions. God is three Persons and we are individual (but also corporate—our gathering and belonging to each other as body or family is part of what it means to be the image of God).

We have several aids that can help us overcome what would otherwise be impossible obstacles to relationship with an unknowable God. These helps can all be classified as *revelation*. For example, the **Bible** is one way that God is revealed to us. The scripture is a collection of historical records of God's interaction with God's people over thousands of years. It is a revelation of who God is and what God thinks and feels.

The Bible provides us with another revelation of God, because it contains the record of *Jesus' life and words*. In Jesus, God took on the full human experience and showed us how to live with God and with each other. Studying Jesus' words and actions is a tremendous help in knowing God.

The scripture also points us to another revelation of God—*the church*, the gathered people of God. Within the scripture, we have the record of the development of the early church, as guided by godly men and women who were listening closely and responding to God. We can read how Spirit-led believers dealt with the historical situations that they encountered, how they were able to build a corporate relationship to God.

We learn from the scripture that the community of believers reveals God to each other and to the world. Part of this is that to be human, male and female, is to be in the image of God. We see some of God when we see each other.

> Then God said, "Let Us make man in Our image, according to Our likeness....And God created man in His own image, in the image of God He created him; male and female He created them.
> (Genesis 1:26-27)

In addition to the natural revelation of God that is in our very humanity, the revelation of God occurs even more meaningfully when God's people gather—for any reason, not just for worship. Jesus says that when two or three

> Nikki: "I've been finding God's image in unbelievers just as much as in Christians. I'm not sure how to react to that."

of us gather, He is there in our midst (Matthew 18:20). He doesn't mean that we should leave an empty chair for Him to sit on. Our very gathering is a revelation of Jesus. We are His body. When people see the gathered church, they see God.

Of course this revelation of God through His people can be seen in a particularly powerful way when God's people express love and worship to Him, and that is interconnected with another form of revelation—*the Holy Spirit.*

One of the main jobs of the Holy Spirit is to dwell in the people of God (in individual believers, of course, but also in the gathered community) and to aid us in building relationship between the human and the divine. That is why God sent the Holy Spirit to the followers of Jesus on the day of Pentecost. All believers have the Spirit dwelling in them and helping them to know and understand God. When we gather, we wait on God corporately as well, listening, paying attention, expecting that the Holy Spirit will tell us the mind and heart of God.

Reflect: Have each person select one of the aids for knowing God (Bible, Jesus, church, Holy Spirit). Put in your own words how this aid has impacted (or could impact) your relationship to God. After the whole group has shared, go back to any of the aids that were not mentioned yet and discuss them as well.

An interactive relationship with God

So, we as the body of Christ, are challenged to develop an interactive relationship with God. I've already spent some time sadly describing how one-sided the typical gathering of believers is. We make a lot of noise in church, most of it beautiful noise. Worship is typically seen as something we do *to* God, towards God. Of course, there is nothing wrong with offering our worship to God—it is what God created us to do. But often we stop there, leaving God no room to speak to or act toward us. We do all the talking.

In fact, think about how Americans surround themselves with noise. When I come home from work I listen to radio in the car, and then turn it on at home while fixing supper. Countless homes have television on all day long. Even those Christians who avoid the invasion of their lives in the form of the TV are often in the habit of having Christian music playing at all times, everywhere they go. My neighbors sit on the porch with their car stereo blasting. People are out jogging through the woods, listening to their iPods and blocking the birdsong, a steady soundtrack filling their senses.

> Stacey: *"In essence the iPod generation becomes self-focused and impersonal. It breaks down community."*

None of these sources of noise are bad in themselves, but we need to be aware that we are using them and be in control of the situation. Why do I want that soundtrack to fill my senses? Do we watch TV and listen to our radio or iPod in order to avoid talking to each other, to avoid having to deal with internal issues in our personal lives?

To avoid hearing the voice of God?

So, in church we talk to God and tell God of our love for Him, and of our thankfulness for what He has done for us. And we keep talking, singing, praying, the whole time we are together. The leaders have made a plan to fill the entire gathering time, to avoid awkward pauses. There is no empty space for listening, no openness for a spontaneous change of direction. Could it be that our worship is indicative of

Ashok: *"My biggest breakthrough in my personal walk with Jesus has been through silent waiting before him."*

a dysfunctional corporate relationship to God? Do we sing and talk the whole time we are gathered in order to avoid listening to Him? Are we afraid of what God might say or do if we were to leave some open space? Are we afraid of what we might learn about ourselves? Or is it that we hardly

Dan: *"I am afraid of silence. I pray that this would change."*

know God at all and are keeping our distance rather than daring to invest in the relationship?

Reflect: How would you answer these questions at this stage in your journey with God?

I hope you believe in a God who speaks to His people. But that doesn't mean that you have been taught the relational skills that would help you towards excellence in this sort of interaction with God. The second half of this book will provide you with some assistance, both for yourself and in case you are a leader who is able to help others. But first, let's come back to the idea of church as family.

The Family Reunion

Something that has helped me to switch away from thinking of our weekly gathering as a sort of program that needs to be planned out and performed each Sunday morning is to use the terminology of *family reunion*. This metaphor is not perfect, as you will realize if you start to use it, but it helps tremendously to change attitudes and expectations. Think of it this way: You are part of a large extended family that is in the habit of hanging out several times a week in various smaller groupings. Once a week the family makes an effort to get everyone together.

> Carina: *"I've moved a lot as an adult, and my church has always functioned as my family. This doesn't mean that I get along with everyone or agree with everyone, but I trust them. I need their different perspectives and I need them to see me for who I really am — good and bad — and for them to tell me what they see so I can keep growing."*

What do families always do when they gather? They eat! Food was central to the gatherings of the early church, and there is no reason why it should not be now. I know that there are women who at this very minute are shaking their heads, knowing the amount of work this would cost them. Well, matriarchs of the family, maybe it's time you truly become mothers to the young people of the church and teach *them* how to cook and clean and set a beautiful table. Maybe it is time for you adult men to be serious about being role models to the young by being the first ones to grab a dish cloth or cook a casserole. If we were all fighting for chances to help and serve, regular meals would not be a burden on anyone.

What else do families do when they gather? They chat, they play games, they discuss serious issues. They laugh together, weep together. The mothers and fathers among us accept their responsibility to rebuke and encourage and teach life skills. The kids get up in front of everyone and sing a song or put on a skit that they've invented. We look at their paintings or book reports or inventions and praise them for their talent.

> Carina: "My grandmother routinely used family meals to gently instruct all of us in table manners, etiquette, and good public behavior"

Every family has "problem people," whether they are simply quirky personalities or people with serious difficulties with sin, addiction, results of abuse, mental health issues, etc. What does a healthy family do? Well, they might roll their eyes or shake their heads at some of the behavior. When necessary, they rebuke and discipline. They lay down the law. But they do not reject their brother or sister. They surround and protect this "unseemly" member.

Now I'm going to shock you. Healthy families gossip! Let me explain. It is a myth born of our extreme American individualism that we ought never to talk about other people. This false understanding of privacy simply serves to drive gossip underground, making it destructive, while at the same time preventing God's people from the normal healthy sort of talk that families ought to do about each other.

How many times have you heard the complaint that Christians use prayer requests as an excuse to gossip about others? Could it be that the need to talk about the friend is genuine, but that we have created no healthy forum for this to occur? Our community should be intimate enough that the adults would agonize together over a young person who is being influenced into harmful behaviors. The family needs to discuss a strategy for dealing with Aunt Helen, who has been telling lies about Aunt Jeannie. The family needs to rally around Uncle Greg, who has lost his job and is in despair. How can we know the needs of the community if we do not talk about each other?

Obviously I do not mean the sort of malicious gossip that the scripture clearly condemns as sin. Rather, a healthy amount of talk and openness can serve to prevent or circumvent the more secretive and destructive behaviors that otherwise might occur.

Reflect: Try applying these descriptions of extended family to the church. What would church be like if it took the family reunion as its pattern?

Being at home with your family

And now, let me tell you a story about visiting people's homes. When I was a campus missionary in Germany as a young single woman, I was often invited to the homes of my students for Christmas or other occasions. My German hosts were always gracious and concerned for my well-being, but you could tell that there was a bit of perfectionism in their mindset about home life. The house was always spotless. The hosts would show me to my room, give me a tour of the home, sit me down on the sofa for pleasant conversation, serve me wonderful meals, cater to my every need. In fact, I felt a bit smothered and wished for some free time to myself. But they had the whole time all planned out.

On the other hand, I also frequently traveled to Freiburg to visit my friends, the Norwoods. As I came through the door, Daphne would say, "same room as last time," and I would carry my bags up and settle myself in, and then wander about the garden or sit and read a book. In the mornings, I'd walk down to the bakery and buy pretzels and crusty rolls, bring them back, and have a cozy breakfast with Daphne until the next daily task called her away. I worked for hours each day in their garden because Daphne was always overwhelmed with kids and ministry responsibilities, and garden work was a vacation activity for me. Sometimes I would hang out with Daphne in the midst of her daily life, other times I would withdraw to do my own thing. When meals were ready someone would holler up the stairs to come and get it. You never knew how many would appear at mealtime. There were always guests coming and going.

Which do you think felt more like home—the perfect program that was planned to the minute, or the chaotic make-yourself-at-home and hang out as you please? Which place do you think I went back to again and again? I of course enjoyed staying with the German families, but I *loved* going to the Norwoods and wanted to return as often as possible, and I knew I could show up just about any time, even without invitation.

Discuss: Can you tell some stories about homes where you've felt welcome?

If the church becomes more like a happy chaotic loving family, we will not be perfect, but we will be attractive to outsiders. If they are used to watching a show when they visit a church, we might be a bit of a shock to them at first. But as long as we envelop them in the family, include them in the daily life, give them a role of their own, new folks will quickly feel that they belong.

This family atmosphere is particularly important for people who are seeking God. I have witnessed repeatedly how a pre-Christian has been welcomed into healthy hearty fellowship and

Annie: "Seems like this would be difficult to implement in a larger church"

treated like one of the family long before they made a final decision for God. Often, they integrate so well that they realize after awhile that they have become a follower of Jesus but can't point to an exact date of "conversion." They have been surrounded by God's people, who are, after all, a revelation of God, and the pathway to trust in God has been so natural that it happened almost without notice. And now that they have come to faith they are already blended into the family of faith, making it much more likely that they will grow to robust maturity.

Paradigms for Worship Gatherings

The previous chapter explored how our relationships with each other and in healthy families can teach us more about our individual and corporate relationships with God. With this in mind, I'd like for us to return now to a discussion of how Christians tend to behave in our gatherings and what healthy developments might be possible.

I have found it helpful to describe some *paradigms* or patterns of worship gatherings that are typical in the western world by using different sorts of musical presentation styles.

1 – The Concert Paradigm

This is currently the most practiced paradigm in non-liturgical churches. The church gathering is organized much like a concert. A more or less talented worship band is stationed at the front, normally on a platform and plugged in. They have chosen the songs and other elements of the musical part of the gathering, they have practiced the program together in advance, and they always follow their plan. The "worship band" is the center of attention in the gathering. If they are good at what they do, they often inspire admiration and create an enjoyable experience for the audience. If they are not very talented or polished, the audience may go home grumbling.

Worship bands tend to be loud, as is befitting a concert. Sometimes they are so loud that members of the audience cannot hear their neighbors or even themselves singing. The concert style of "service" normally results in at best a sing-along, and at worst a passive audience who simply observes as the band "worships" and gives their assent to what is happening.

Churches that follow the concert paradigm typically follow up the worship band performance with a monologue speech, called a sermon. Again, the emphasis is on delivery, professionalism, and even entertainment. Because it is understood to have a performance element to it, the sermon is subject to audience scrutiny. (How many times have you heard a response like, "He put me to sleep this morning," or "She really knows how to keep people interested.")

What's good about this paradigm? The best of these worship bands make beautiful and/or exciting music, and they can be enjoyable to watch. Surely it is a good thing to see people making music to God and enjoying it. Just like attending a concert, you can be swept up emotionally and feel that you have shared a significant experience with those around you. Similarly, a well-crafted and -delivered sermon can be inspirational.

What's not-so-good? Well, the audience is just that—an audience. The concert

> Bree: "'Making judgments.' This is me in a typical worship time."

paradigm creates passivity, people who listen but do not participate (are they truly worshipping if they are not singing or speaking?), who feel inadequate because they are not equally talented, or who wish to someday be the ones to be up front leading/performing/receiving attention. If God is expected to speak, it is through the worship leaders and the pastor's sermon. We hope they are listening to God for us. The performance feel causes the audience to make judgments—positive or negative—about the skill of the band and the preacher, and whether it was all done in the "right" style.

2 – The Big Band/Symphony Paradigm

Again, this type of gathering is strongly directed from the front, with one person in leadership of the musical part of worship. Here, however, whatever musical instruments are employed are seen as supporting the entire congregation, which is considered to be producing the worship music. It is as if each person were an instrument in a band or orchestra. The leader, like a band director, gives strong direction—when to sit or stand, when to be loud or quiet, when there should be solos or accents on different instruments (e.g., only the men sing, or only the women).

> Jim: "This has its time and place for building corporate unity."

The congregation understands themselves to be performing together for God, making a joyful noise unto the "audience of One." There are non-liturgical churches that more or less follow this paradigm, and most liturgical ones would fit here.

The sermon may be as described above for the concert paradigm. Some emerging churches, however, have developed a method of teaching that meshes well with this more interactive and participatory paradigm. The pastor may sit in the middle of a circled congregation or at the front, but is likely to alternate speaking and interaction with the people. There may be a question and answer time, or the pastor may ask people for ideas—keeping their minds more actively engaged with the material. The people feel that they are helping the pastor, that all of them are learning together.

What's good? In this paradigm, there is more recognition of the giftedness of the body, that each person plays a part. It is more likely that the people remember what was said and sung when they go home, because their minds were actively engaged. They are likely to feel that they matter as individuals, that the gathering would have been different if they had not been there. They are therefore also less likely to "judge" the quality or success of the gathering as if they were simply an audience.

What's not-so-good? Unless it is actively counteracted, the big band paradigm still tends not to encourage authentic interaction among the people. There is still a plan to be followed, and if God wishes to speak it would be mostly limited to the leadership, especially during worship, which is strongly led from the front.

3 – The Jazz Band Paradigm

Now, I am not a big fan of jazz music.[45] But the way a jazz band plays together makes for a great illustration of unity with diversity. As with the big band paradigm, the people are the instruments. Each of them is essential, playing in harmony with the others. But this time, though there is human leadership and organization of the gathering, it is less obvious, less dominant. Think about how a jazz band functions.

As a jazz piece is being played, any member of the band can add something, and the others welcome the new impulse and respond accordingly. There will be a common thread, a repeated theme, a focus, a goal. But there is also the adventure of not knowing exactly what is going to happen next. Every time the band plays together new things happen in the midst of the established patterns. The group strives for excellence and unity by practicing together, but continues to desire and be open to

---

[45] My favorites are bluegrass, folk, and world music, which, when you think about it, are often played in much the same way as jazz. You could also use a rock-and-roll jam session to describe this paradigm.

innovation, creativity, and experimentation. This creates an alertness and an awareness of individual responsibility.

> Heather: "I was involved with Jazz Band for 5 years (8th-12th grade). I learned to love it! Everyone had their own part in the 'performance.' Even if our musical part wasn't 'cool' or the main melody, it was still essential to the whole. Background music is just as or even more important than the soloist's part. My band director would always say, 'We're as good as our weakest "link" or member.' Everyone is important. Also, yeah there was a band-leader, but he'd often step back and let us go with it. His leadership was present but really was less visible, often only starting the song or finishing it."

Now think of how this paradigm could describe a charismatic gathering of Christians. There would be leaders who have prayed and made some plans, and who are able to give needed guidance. But the expectation would be on all the members to take part as the Holy Spirit prompts them. Let's say that there are several musical instruments to assist in singing, perhaps in front or perhaps interspersed in the gathering. In fact, they might be the voices of gifted singers. The musical instruments would be seen as giftings that assist in musical worship, but not the dominant impulse-givers.

Instead, the leaders would make sure there are several times of quiet waiting on God. During such a time, someone might read a scripture out loud, another might pray. Someone else might start singing a song and everyone else would join in. Another person might stand up and say that s/he feels like God wants us to pray for a particular situation, or that the Spirit is impressing on him/her that the worship should focus on an aspect of God's character. Any of these new impulses could cause the gathering to change direction. The classical elements of musical worship and sermon or teaching would be possible impulses in obedience to the Spirit, but not necessary in every gathering.

What's good about this paradigm? First of all this type of gathering fits very nicely with the description Paul gave in I Cor 14:26, as well as the theological concepts of the body, the giftedness of believers, and the Spirit wishing to reveal God's heart and mind to and through the congregation. The members would be seeking to be in unity with each other and with the theme that the Spirit is weaving amongst them, yet at the same time each of them would feel personal responsebility for hearing from God for the building up of the body.

> Jim: "College students fall away because they haven't learned (in youth services) to hear from God for themselves."

There would be an alertness and openness. People would come to each gathering wondering what God was going to do in their midst and what their own part might be.

What's not-so-good? It isn't that there is much wrong with this paradigm at all, but that we have forgotten how to do it (or—more likely—never imagined such a thing to be possible). Teaching, training, and good leadership would be essential. A church that embarks on this journey is sure to have gatherings during which things get chaotic or when it all just falls flat. The jazz paradigm is harder work for leaders—at least in the early days. It is much easier to plan a performance and follow a same old same old pattern than to bring a group of people together for

> Anita: "How do you lead but also let the Holy Spirit lead? I don't think we really train people for that kind of leadership."

something more spontaneous and unpredictable. Pastors could feel nervous, and the people could feel some amount of insecurity if they aren't sure whether the pastor will be able to handle things.

Reflect: Which of the three worship paradigms best describes the church or group you belong to? What is your response to my evaluation of these paradigms? Can you think of other paradigms?

Is the jazz paradigm even possible?

You might be skeptical. You've never experienced anything like this and can't imagine it working in your church. I'm happy to tell you that I've seen it repeatedly in different cultures, different denominations, and different age groups. It does take dedication from the leadership, but if they are truly convinced of the biblical principles and do a good job of helping their people grow into a fuller expression of the charismata, such spontaneous interactive gatherings can become almost effortless.

Some real life examples

Let me describe to you several gatherings for worship that I have experienced.[46] Please note that these gatherings developed over time. They were groups of believers who were clearly taught and effectively discipled.

Christians in Action University Church, USA (early 1980s)

About 300 young adults gather Sunday evenings for lively, passionate worship. One evening, as we pause expectantly between songs, a member of the church spontaneously reads a scripture that deeply touches a number of others. They begin to pray out loud in response. Clearly, the Spirit is working on this aspect in many people's lives. The leadership, sitting together near

---

[46] I have combined occurrences of these groups into composites for the sake of brevity, but all of these things really happened. Indeed, the examples given were not exceptional but typical.

the front, listens to what God is saying through the scripture and the prayers, consults, and decides to skip the planned sermon and continue on with singing and prayer in alignment with this unexpected theme.

Another time, as the musical worship time begins, there is a heavy feeling, as if the people just can't sing. The leaders decide to move straight to the sermon, which turns out to be a prophetic word that speaks to people's hearts and moves them to a ministry time, followed by a time of singing that is free and heartfelt.

Christians in Action meets every Sunday morning for intercession. This is not your basic take-turns-saying-nice-wishes-to-God prayer meeting. We normally pray more than an hour for only one topic. The leadership team, made up of people who are especially gifted at intercessory prayer, has waited on God for a topic, and researched it in preparation for the gathering. After a time of musical worship and centering on God, they introduce the topic and the whole group takes it before God, praying together in unknown languages for a while as we seek to know the heart of God for this situation. Then people share impressions they have received that may help us to know how to pray. Sometimes this is matter-of-fact, sometimes deeply emotional, but it is always profoundly prophetic and therefore exciting. We are making a real difference in the physical and spiritual worlds.

As a beginner at this sort of prayer, I am normally quiet, but I try to listen to the Spirit and I search my Bible, hoping to find a verse that fits the direction of the prayer. Sometimes I gather my courage and read a verse out loud. It is encouraging to me to see how the others take hold of the words of scripture that I read and incorporate them into the prayer. I am learning that I, too, can hear from God.

Students For Christ, Germany (early 1990s)

I lead a ministry of around 50 young adults, of whom 8-10 are in a leadership core. On this particular evening we are singing worship songs, led on acoustic guitar by Sonja, and supported by Dominik with his guitar. We pause to wait on God. One of the members prays and others follow suit, clearly deeply moved by the Holy Spirit. The theme appears to be repentance—an entirely different direction than Sonja had planned. How to follow this up with an appropriate song that will take the theme seriously? Sonja and Dominik each have a chord book with several hundred songs. As people are continuing to pray, the guitarists are quietly paging through the book, asking God to show them the right musical response. Then they notice a hand motion from Reinhard, who is running the overhead projector (remember those?), and has all the songs available in front of him as well. He holds one overhead up and they instantly recognize that it is the right one for the moment. As the prayer subsides, they begin to sing the song. After that song, Julia, who is sitting in the congregation, leads out with her voice in another song that continues the thread perfectly.

Another evening in the middle of prayer, a young man stands up and begins to sort of pray-rant. It is clearly not from God, but he is on the other side of the room. I am considering whether to correct him from the front or walk over to him when Martin appears at his side, touching his elbow and guiding him out of the room. Because the congregation is experienced, they do not feel insecure at such interruptions because they know that the leadership will deal with it appropriately.

St Stephens Church, England (late 1990s)

I am a member of the leadership team for the charismatic evening service of this Anglican church. The vicar has pulled the team together, but he trusts us, rarely attends our planning meetings, and does not assert authority over the team (ranging in age from 25 to 60). In fact, none of us is designated as leader of the team. The church administrator helps to keep us organized because that is his gifting, but the rest of the team is made up of talented musician-pastors and preacher-teachers. There are no power plays, and no one dominates, even when there are minor disagreements on strategy. We try to hear the voice of God, we talk things out, we compromise. Some of us are adventurous, others more cautious, but we are all passionate for God to be honored and therefore willing to step out in new things. A special anointing seems to be on this team, with the result that the gatherings we lead on Sunday evenings, though in form more like the symphony paradigm, are without pretense, full of passionate worship and prayer response, and clearly effective in changing lives.

Reflect: Share some of your own real life examples that were similar to the ones I've given above.

Tra-di-SHUN!

So, why is something like the jazz band paradigm not happening in most Christian gatherings? You may have heard someone blame church traditions for the lack of freedom. Is *tradition* the problem?

Tradition is frequently a dirty word among more innovative groups. You often find people who grew up in a liturgical church who are desperate for more freedom in worship. Yet at the same time, I am aware of a large movement of young evangelicals and pentecostals who are flocking to the

> Nikki: "I find some liturgies to be beautiful, but other traditions to be dead. I think that something may start out beautiful, so people want to hang on to it, but after doing the same thing hundreds of times it loses its meaning."

111

liturgical churches out of hunger for depth of meaning, mystery, and wonder.

Yes, a stubborn perpetuation of any sort of tradition for tradition's sake can be a cause of frustration for hungry, adventurous believers. But traditions can also be rich and full of meaning. Traditions are, after all, the jewels crystallized out of powerful experiences of the presence of God in past generations.

Indeed, any group of followers of Jesus should strive to tap into all sorts of wonderful ways to worship that have resulted from past renewal and devotion. In Students for Christ-Germany, we tried to make use of the faith traditions of our members. These ranged from choosing worship choruses that follow the Lutheran liturgy to reciting the creeds to waiting in silence as in a Quaker meeting to the dynamic rhythm of black gospel churches, and much more. It is because groups of Christians have developed liturgies and traditions that we have these rich resources to draw from.

Reflect: If you have been to a liturgical church, discuss how it impacted you—whether positively or negatively. What traditions do you recognize in your own church? How did they arise?

No, the problem is not tradition. The problem is *routinization.* Have a look at the drawing on the next page

Most revival and renewal movements, large and small, follow this cycle. It goes like this: Imagine a denomination, individual church, or sub-group of believers that has been in a well-established routine for a long time. This may be a liturgical church, an evangelical Bible church, or a lively praise band church. But some of

> Heather: "If leadership is tired, they will want to go into maintenance because it's less for them to do."

the members are unhappy. They can't really explain why, but they feel restless. They may describe their dissatisfaction with such statements as "I'm not being fed," "I just don't feel God's presence," "It's boring," or "There must be more than this." These are symptoms of a church that is either in the *maintenance* stage or the *routinization* stage. What used to be a new and exciting way of worshipping God has become same old, same old. The forms had originally come into being because they were meaningful, but that meaning has been lost.

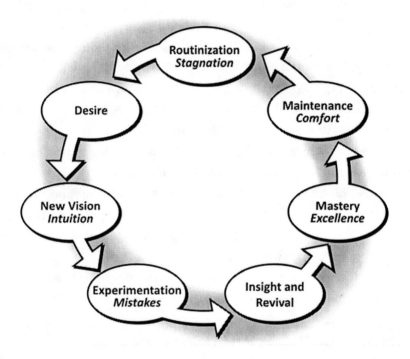

This group of believers is actually at an exciting juncture, full of possibilities. Depending on their maturity level and the openness of the leadership to support them, they might turn into a bunch of complainers, they might leave to look for something that fits them better, or they might take the church on an adventure with God that leads to renewal and revival.

As they act on their *desire* for a deeper experience with God, or more meaningful community, or whatever they perceive to be missing, these people will study their Bibles, pray, interact with each other and with outsiders, and gain new *vision* into what other possibilities are out there. They will *experiment*.[47] Some experiments will fall flat, others will have uncomfortable results. This is a critical juncture. An insecure leadership might at this point say, "Whoa, this is too scary. Let's go back to our safe secure old ways of doing things." But a confident leader with mature people will be able to say, "Well, that didn't work. Let's talk about why and see if our evaluation might help us find a different path that will bring us to our goal."

> Aaron: "We must recognize that this temporary discomfort leads to a deeper knowledge of God."

The courage to face the difficulties and to learn from them can result in *insight* and further experimentation, eventually leading to true *revival*. Over and over throughout church history, people who set out on such a search for renewed relationship to God have found it, and these new forms of community and worship have either revived existing structures or become new denominations. Newly formed denominations, in particular, often develop a gathering and leadership structure based on the experiences that they have had and that have given meaning to their pilgrimage. And so revival becomes a source of new traditions.

Every tradition is the result of revival entering the *mastery* mode. This creates a rich heritage. If you are a leader, your goal should be to keep your people moving between *desire* and *mastery*.

---

[47] As I write this book, there is a Pentecostal church in the Twin Cities that is sponsoring an Episcopal-type liturgical service once a month. They are experimenting with something that a number of Christians in the area are feeling a need for. Who knows what will result from this?

In this way you will continue to draw from that rich heritage and honor it while at the same time filling it with renewed meaning and adventure.

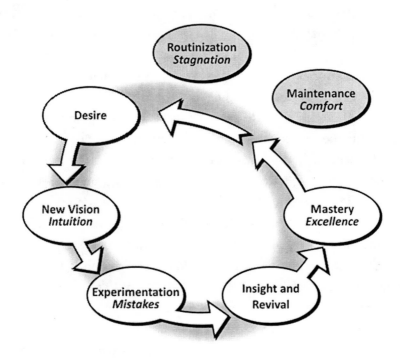

Discuss: At what stage in the cycle would you put your congregation? What might this mean for future strategies and plans? How can you support your church in this process?

Avoiding routinization

From the description above, you will recognize that it is not tradition (or mastery), but *routinization* that a leader must be watching for and strategizing against.

This is not an easy task. Constant renewal takes vigilance and a refusal to rest on your laurels. Many years ago I heard a successful university pastor say that whenever something starts to work well in his ministry, he starts to look for a new thing to replace it. I was impressed by this statement and tried to employ it in my own ministry. But it was also not surprising to meet him years later—still successful—and learn that he had forgotten he'd ever made that statement, settled into a pattern, and had no plans to change it. It is much easier to lead a ministry that has settled into a comfortable groove than to always be alert to the Spirit's guidance into a new experience with God.

The question that a leader must ask concerning tradition has to do with the *current reality* of the interaction between God and God's people. Is the presence of God clearly felt by most of the people in the gathering? Is what we are doing and experiencing *real* or is it hype or is it an empty form? If there is no reality, then the group is spending too much time in the maintenance mode, losing the vitality, and in danger of stagnation.

This certainly does not mean that every gathering of believers must cause goose-bumps. Remember we said that relationship to God is a lot like relationship to other people? Well, think of the couple who have been married 20 years or more. They have long periods of simply being comfortable with each other. There is nothing wrong with a body of believers developing a worship tradition that feels safe and comforting.

The problem comes when the routine is all there is. The married couple who have no surprises in their relationship, who don't argue anymore because they are so good at avoiding truth, who are simply living out their days in parallel paths without much actual interaction, are not demonstrating a good marriage! We don't want our corporate (or our individual) relationship to God to be like that. We want there to be a spark, some friction, some discomfort or surprises to keep us growing and alive and in love.

Reflect: List off areas where you see routinization in your daily life, your relationships, your work, and your spiritual life.

It's about the revelation of God

Overcoming routinization is not about rejecting tradition, but rather determining to continually fill the tradition with fresh meaning. Routinization describes a group of believers who have "settled," and who no longer deliberately seek the revelation of God. If the gatherings of a church are boring—and boring can happen whether the routine is quiet and dignified or loud and boisterous—then the revelation of God is not occurring. When God is being revealed, it will not be boring. How could it be?!

One might expect that routinization could be avoided within the Charismatic/Pentecostal movements. These are people who say that they expect God to speak in their midst. The sad fact is, however, that these groups are just as likely to routinize their gatherings as any other group. Remember that human tendency to seek comfort and safety? Well, Pentecostal groups also settle into routines. If you were to visit many of the historic Pentecostal churches today, their gatherings would not appear different from any evangelical church.

> Kris: "If we want to break the routine, will we be accused of being rebellious?"

If these "settled" Pentecostal churches do experience apparent manifestations of the Spirit, they tend to occur less often, or perhaps they take on a predictable (routinized) pattern—the same person praying the same prayer or having the same "word from God" week after week, the same "order of service," a failure to learn new songs or incorporate new instruments or ways of worshipping. People stop being alert, stop feeling personally responsible to hear from God, stop truly interacting with God as a gathered body. If the same routine happens every time believers meet, and a revelation of God is no longer occurring, then God's voice is being blocked out of the gatherings even if the people pray in unknown languages and have lively music.

The determining factor for a church that is truly pentecostal is not worship style, it is not tradition or liturgy, it is not energy level. The determining factor is the revelation of God. Any church from any denominational background can be pentecostal and charismatic. The Holy Spirit will reveal the heart and mind of God when God's people are listening and responding. God's people will listen and respond if the leaders teach them how, encourage, model, correct, give room for God to speak, and avoid routinization.

Reflect: Do you want to see this in your church? Does such a direction make you feel excited or anxious? Or are there other emotions? Explain.

Leading Change

If you are like me, you are hungry, even starving, for genuine encounters with the living God in the midst of His people. When you discuss such topics as we've developed above, your heart burns within you and you just want everything to change all at once. I would like to give you hope, but I also want to caution you. This book would fail if it were to set you up for frustration.

If you are a pastor, you may find yourself agreeing with the material in this book but baffled as to how to move your people from their current complacency to the point of being active worshippers and integrated members of the body. I'm not going to give you all the answers to all the problems, but the second half of the book is intended to help you learn to strategize and bring about healthy growth in yourself and in the people of God for whom you have responsibility.

Change is hard work, so pray

You can't move a group of people into an interactive mode without some important elements. The first one is always prayer. Only the Holy Spirit can bring about true, deep, healthy growth in people. Only He can cause that desire to develop inside them that will give them the courage to experiment and step out into unknown territory, to take risks in their relationships to God and to each other. Devoting ourselves to earnest, seeking prayer will serve to align our hearts with the heart of God, opening us to new things, and helping us to become more immediately responsive to the Holy Spirit's voice amongst us.

You might be praying alone for a while, but it is rare to find a church where only one person is hungry for more of God's presence. Normally you will soon come across others who feel the same way, and you will be able to pray together, encourage and advise each other, and begin practicing being charismatic and pentecostal in your small gathering.

Reflect: Do you know of other people who have the same desire to see God move and speak in your gatherings? What healthy steps could you take to join hearts and vision with them?

Avoid spiritual elitism

When a group of people are seeking hard after God while others are either unaware, cautious, or rejecting, there is a dangerous tendency toward judgmentalism and elitism. If you find yourself part of a group that is beginning to speak in terms of "us" vs. "them," then you are treading on thin ice. Please don't be pulled into this. The only reason to seek after God is for the good of the *whole* body. You may feel rejected by the rest of the church because you are being too pushy or not explaining yourself well. Back off, take your time, be gentle and patient.

Reflect: Can you share any experiences of spiritual elitism in the past, and what effect it had on the church where it occurred?

The pastor's job is to teach and train

We will start expanding on effective strategy below, but if you are a pastor, you must begin with persuasive teaching and gentle guidance.

Some churches have a mix of gifted people, previous experience, and maturity that will allow them to embrace new vision and begin living it out quickly with a minimum of guidance and training. But most will be cautious and skeptical.

Teaching is an important key to change. One of the biggest mistakes that pastors make is to try to change a church too quickly and without enough explanation. Many admirable new initiatives in churches fail simply because the leadership did not take the time to prepare the congregation. The best idea, presented too suddenly or forced upon people, will create resentment and is almost certain to be sabotaged.

A church is not a machine that can be steered at will. Even with good teaching, you must be prepared for slow, thoughtful, foundational growth. You will also have changeover in membership, with new members bringing both gifts and challenges, so that your strategy will need to shift over time. And truly, no church will ever "arrive" at some sort of perfect interactive relationship with God.

But good-hearted people will be willing to take risks if they understand what, why, and how. If their hearts are towards God, they will be glad for a pastor who is helping them learn how to grow closer to Him.

Reflect: Are you a "good-hearted" person? What do you need from your pastor to help you grow and take risks?

Block out a period of time to teach on ecclesiology. Help people realize that there is so much more they could be doing to develop a healthy corporate relationship to God. Point out how your current church model is good, but not complete. Make use of the biblical pictures of family, body, priesthood, etc.

Don't just *talk* about it in theoretical terms, but find ways to use the one or two hours you are together on Sunday mornings to guide people into self-discovery. Try discussion groups based on well-thought-out questions, team projects and testimony times that help people to know (and therefore love) each other better, or guided prayer or worship times structured much like a workshop, including feedback afterwards. Have brain-storming sessions with the entire congregation to draw out their ideas on how to be more like family, or how to better practice being priests for one another. Continually search for creative ways to emphasize community and belonging to one another, forgiveness and patience,[48] and a healthy understanding of the role of leadership.

There may be some benefit to starting with a core group of yielded people and/or leaders that meets outside of the main weekly gathering, but while that group is meeting and developing a closer relationship with God and each other, be sure you continue to use the sort of methods described above to teach and equip the whole body. Otherwise you could end up with the elitism problem I mentioned earlier.

Challenge people to embrace the fact that getting close to God and to each other can be uncomfortable. In much the same way that a marriage counselor might encourage a couple to break out of their established patterns in order to deepen their relationship,

---

[48] Virtues like forgiveness and patience become all the more important as a church moves into deeper experience of God and of community. Churches where people don't know each other rarely see personality conflicts and bad behavior. But when you start being family, you will see the sides of people that you didn't know about, and everyone will need to be taught how to love and accept one another, warts and all.

explain to your people that their corporate relationship to God

> Jim: "When we always do the same things, we lose the sense of needing to hear from God."

needs to be continually evolving and maturing. Help them understand that avoiding risk as a church may lead to stagnation and to believers who never reach maturity.

At the same time, free your church from the pressure to be perfect. They will grow in discernment through making mistakes. Impress upon them that it is okay to experiment, that it is okay to try and fail. Failure should be presented as a learning experience that may open the pathway to something wonderful and unexpected. Remember, the goal is to keep the church moving from desire to mastery and back to desire without lapsing into maintenance and routinization. Rather than aiming for some "perfect" expression of the church, communicate that you plan to grow and change until Jesus comes back!

Reflect: Are you more likely to be a person who is pushing for change or a person who is cautious? What are the strengths and weaknesses of your personality type?

Finally, and this can feel alarming to a pastor, but you need to be prepared to lose some folks. There will be those for whom growth and closer relationships is too threatening. Be gentle with them. Listen to them. But do not let them set the agenda. Realize that you will never please everyone. It is much more important to support the members who are itching for a new adventure with God than to placate those who hold back in spite of good teaching and a healthy process. If people do leave, make every effort to send them away with blessing and a positive attitude.

The Worship Gathering—Let's Get Practical

Remember that the way we worship teaches theology. If we get stuck on a form for form's (or convenience') sake, we will teach believers that God is only pleased with people who follow our particular routine, or that this routine is the only way to know God. Our tradition may be rooted in a rich history, but if it is not filled with the current revelation of God, but has become empty and meaningless; people will wonder if God is even present. If

> Carina: "God made ALL of our being, and intends for our whole self to be part of worshipping him."

we do not engage the whole person—mind, emotions, body, and spirit—people will subconsciously think that worshipping God is only about the part of our humanity that is emphasized in their church. In some types of gatherings they might end up equating relationship to God purely to an emotional response; in others they might think it is only about intellectual assent to a set of creedal statements.

As you guide people into growth in community and in corporate worship, always be asking yourself, "What does this (method or experience or emphasis) teach us about God and about our relationship with God?"

> Mike: "God is a God of order, but also a God of creativity. Ask God to show you creative ways to do church, as well as strategies for implementing these ideas."

Reflection: Do you tend to be someone who desires emotional experience, or someone who likes an intellectual challenge? Talk about why it is important to have both types of people in a church body. How do diverse personalities help each other to know God better?

Teaching People to be Active in Worship Gatherings

I'm going to direct this section to pastors and other leaders, because ultimately it has to be about leaders equipping the saints—helping the whole church with all its diverse members to grow up into the fullness of Christ. However, if you are an individual member of a church you can still learn from what you read here. At the very least it will help you understand and support what your pastor is doing.[49]

It is one thing for a leader to decide that s/he would like God's people to recognize their giftings and participate more actively in gatherings. It is quite another to facilitate this growth.

As we discussed above, the most important thing you can do, pastor, is to *deepen community* and *pray*. Get to know your people

> Tim: *"That's the essence of Acts 2:4."*

well, pray for and with them, teach them how to love each other, ask the Holy Spirit to give you strategic ideas that are catered to the unique identity of this particular group of people. What has meaning for and causes spiritual growth in another church may not be at all right for yours.

Pay attention to *themes*. Seek out from God what the focus should be, both in the planning times and during worship gatherings. For example, God may want your church to spend weeks or months pursuing holiness,

> Carina: *"The Spirit moves in preparation AND spontaneity."*

embracing joy, more fully understanding the cross, or experiencing more depth to their devotional life in God. As such themes arise in gatherings, point them out to your people and be consistent and strategic in helping the congregation embrace them.

---

[49] And you will have noticed by now that the discussion questions throughout the book are for the regular church members. They will help you to think through and find appropriate responses to what I'm saying to the leaders.

You are the one who must *empower the people* you lead. They will not empower themselves. You may wish with your whole heart for Spirit-filled worship, but if you have not said this out loud and taught about it and modeled it, the people are not likely to leap over you and do it anyway.

> Matt: *"People who complain are powerless people."*

To start with, each member of the leadership team for a gathering should know that s/he has permission to suggest direction. The leaders can become examples to the congregation of what might be possible as a group of believers comes together.

But even more, this permission must be extended to the entire congregation. It must be clear that you, as the leader(s), recognize that God may choose to speak through any member, that you expect it to happen, and that nothing would make you happier. You must free people to share what God is putting on their heart, give them permission to "disrupt" the plan for the gathering if the Holy Spirit so prompts.

Reflect: At this point in the spiritual growth of your church, would you feel comfortable "disrupting" the plan for a gathering if the Holy Spirit were to prompt you? What would help you to step out in this area?

The leader is also the *role model* for biblical worship. It is best to have several leaders modeling the sort of worship you wish the people to grow into. Many of the members will be anxious as to what is expected, and if they see it in you first, they will feel more confidence in stepping out themselves. If you want them to pray out loud, have members of the leadership team do that first. If you want them to learn to dance joyfully before God, the leaders must be the first and most exuberant dancers.

But be careful not to be too far out there. Be one step ahead of your people, but no more. If they are just starting to learn to pray out loud, don't you be entering into intercession with shouting and foot-stamping and rebuking of demons. Be just a bit louder when the congregation learns to pray or sing together in unknown languages. Share a word from

> Mike: "I have learned that the more freely I worship, the more freely the people I'm leading will worship. Sometimes we wait for the spiritual atmosphere to change, when all along we are supposed to be part of the solution."

God just a bit more often than members of the congregation do. Be just a bit freer than others in physically demonstrating your love for God.

Otherwise your example will feel unattainable, or even undesirable, and they will be more likely to back off, to decide not to step out in new skills. Being a role model has a lot to do with encouraging others to go farther than they would on their own. But pray for the day when you have to struggle to keep up with them!

> There they go!
> I must hasten after them,
> for I am their leader.

(Unknown source)

Teach, teach, teach

I know I said this already, but I am determined to impress upon you how important it is. The church has had plenty of preaching. It needs teachers. Often we relegate teaching to the Sunday school,[50] which is attended by only a minority of the

---

[50] Or whatever form your church is using for Christian education.

members. If what is being taught is important, it ought to be taught to all. This means doing less preaching and more teaching in your main gatherings.

As a foundation, your people need to be taught the historical and religious backgrounds of the Bible, as well as how to rightly use scripture. They need to be taught how to do biblical theology.[51] They need to learn of the balance between God's grace in salvation and their call to respond with holy living. They need to understand the difference between matters of conscience (clothing, food, drink, etc.) and truly moral/ethical matters (found in the sin lists, the virtue lists, and other strong clear imperatives in the scripture). And so on.

Reflect: Which topics, background knowledge, or skills need to be taught more in your church? Which are you strong in?

But the members of the church also need to be taught the principles on which you are building the church. Such information is not just for the leadership team. Talk out loud (and frequently!) about your vision and goals for the church, about who they can become in God. Teach them that we have a God who speaks, who

---

[51] I am not a fan of *systematic* theology, which tends to form a framework based on human assumptions about who God is and what God must be like, and then search the Bible for verses to support those assumptions. I would urge you instead to learn to do *biblical* theology, which begins with scripture as a record of God's encounters and interactions with people throughout history, and begins to draw conclusions based on those encounters. Developing a biblical theology is a lifetime work. Church history and the manifestations of the Holy Spirit in the church will also inform us as we build our corporate and individual relationships to God. If you go back and read the sections on what the words "pentecostal" and "charismatic" mean, you will see that this is the method I used to form a theology of the gathered people of God.

expects our attention when He speaks, and that worship is an interactive corporate relationship with God. Use scripture to demonstrate this. As the church grows and draws seekers, provide helps for newcomers to understand what is happening in the gatherings and/or suggest regularly that visitors talk to someone afterwards if they have questions.

Reflect: Can you articulate the vision and goals of your church?

However, teaching is not just "talk." Strategic pastoral guidance, using *various* teaching methods, is one of the biggest lacks in our churches. Sure, the pastor *preaches* plenty. But the people do not need inspiration and talk as much as they need training and insight. They need to internalize and integrate, not just be told what to do and how to think. How to accomplish this?

Be a *strategist*. Evaluate where your people are now, and think of strategies to help them move from point A to point B. Don't be impatient or judgmental, but rather come up with creative ways to empower them. Are folks shy and hesitant to step out because they still don't know each other well? Then you must focus on building community until they begin to love and trust each other. Are they afraid to take risks? Share your own mistakes and fears and hopes of growth with them. Be a fellow learner. Don't give them the impression that you are perfect and have it all figured out, or they will be intimidated. Are people uncertain about speaking out loud during gatherings? Find ways of giving them a voice (reading an assigned scripture, feedback times, guided impression-sharing, requesting song suggestions).

A gifted teacher will look at the situation, the people, and the material that s/he wants the congregation to internalize or put into practice, and then strategize about the most effective way to reach that goal. For example, the sermon is normally *not* the most effective way to bring about growth in people.[52]   You yourself know how often it occurs that when someone asks you—even an hour later—what the latest sermon was about, you cannot bring it back to your mind. In order to make sermons more memorable, pastors tend to fall into the performance mode and make use of jokes, power point slides, and other tricks to keep people's attention.   Why not just admit that sermons are not typically effective and look for a better way?

People have widely varying learning styles. Some do learn by listening, others respond well to visual aids, but by far the majority learn by "doing." These folks need to have their body engaged in some way. In order to impact a group of people with such varying learning styles, you will want to alternate and combine teaching methods regularly in order to keep everyone engaged and moving forward. Yes, use an occasional series of lectures. But use other methods as well: testimonies by members who have already experienced what you want the congregation to learn, discussion times with provocative questions, group brain-storming about the topic, small group assignments, or come up with your own creative ideas.

Reflect: What is your learning style, and what methods have been most successful in convincing you to change and grow?

Do mini-sermons or offer "tidbits" of teaching before and during times of seeking God. If you can resist forcing too much

---

[52] See *Communication Theory for Christian Witness*, by Charles Kraft.   He classifies the sermon as a "monologue speech," and describes the typical worship service as a "ritual of solidarity." In other words, the typical church "service" provides a way for people to express their agreement with the doctrine and behavioral standards of the church, but it is not effective in bringing about real change in those who attend.

information on people at any one time, they are more likely to remember the content. Have workshop-style training sessions in which people try out new skills and talk with each other about the results. Feedback, though highly effective, is one of the least used methods, perhaps because leaders can't control what will be said. But what a powerful learning experience it is when one person shares what they were sensing from God during worship and another says, "Yes, that's exactly how I was feeling too!" In this way they learn to trust what they think they are hearing from God and become more likely to act on similar impressions in the future.

When someone does step out and do something for the first time, s/he needs *affirmation*. Be sure to tell the person afterwards how helpful their gift was to the whole group. Teach your people to do affirmation for each other—if someone shares a word that touches another, the recipient should thank the one who shared. Be sure you, as leader, are taking manifestations of the Spirit seriously. If you lead the gathering in an immediate response to impulses given by the Holy Spirit through church members, they will be encouraged that they have shared something true and significant, something that made a difference.

Do *correction* in public only if something has happened that will cause real trouble. If your congregation is mature, they will

> Phil: "How do we deal with someone who claims to speak a word of God but their lives do not show the fruit and their words bring confusion or control?"

recognize when a behavior is off base and, because they know that you will be taking care of it at an appropriate time, they will be able to shrug it off. But if you have a genuine problem person who is regularly disruptive, then you may have to take public action. Be firm and consistent, and do not hesitate to be drastic if necessary. You should be jealous for the health of the community and not allow an unhealthy person to do damage.

This is not easy to do

Why is it often difficult for leaders to interrupt the flow of a gathering in order to correct or re-direct? One reason is that human beings prefer to avoid conflict, and not many leaders have been equipped with the interpersonal skills needed for strong intervention.

But another likely reason goes back to the worship paradigms. The church gathering is probably being treated and understood as a performance rather than a family get-together. And, after all, it is bad form to interrupt a performance. On the other hand, it is *good* form to insist on proper manners and good attitudes in a family circle. The ability to gather everyone together and talk through what is appropriate, and then return to a time of waiting on God is a strong indication that a church has become a family.

Many times, a church fails to grow in active participation because their leaders are anxious and insecure. Pastoral leaders may find it easier to stick to a performance oriented program in which the congregation is passive than to take the risk of letting people become more active and interactive. A pastor may theoretically support the idea of a charismatic gathering to which all the members bring gifts, but if s/he is nervous or talks too much about potential mistakes, the pastor will pass on this insecurity and reinforce passivity.

Let's have another look at Margaret Poloma's study. Something else that she mentioned was the tension pastors face between the need to correct manifestations that are out of order and the desire to encourage proper charismatic expression.

> A person speaking out with the 'wrong message' or
> engaging in inappropriate affective expressions can cause
> serious problems of order within a Pentecostal service.
> Such experiences have caused some pastors to be wary of
> charismatic expressions and to attempt to hold the lid on

activities that have given Pentecostalism its distinctiveness. A pastor who personally is experientially unfamiliar with prophetic manifestations is likely to be more uncomfortable with congregational manifestations of them.[53]

Indeed, encouraging the whole church to seek the revelation of God as a community may lead to situations in which leaders will have to lead strongly and skillfully.

Pastor, you need to be seeking the revelation of God yourself, so that you are comfortable with it. At the same time, you must be willing to exercise strong but sensitive leadership when necessary. No one will be willing to take a risk if they think you might not be able to deal with it or that you might embarrass them or judge them for a mistake they make.

The paradox of strong leadership

And here is the paradox. Even though the pastor needs to be a strong and strategic leader in order to facilitate pentecostal and charis-matic gatherings, s/he must also be willing to step back and let go of control.

Realize that biblical worship is going to cost something. It will necessarily involve taking risks. When you free people to share their gifts and respond to the prompting of the Holy Spirit in your gatherings, you may

> Mike: "Having grown up in Pentecostal churches and seen both sides, I have come to realize that, despite my fears and mistrust of man "faking" the move of the Holy Spirit, I couldn't reject what was genuine simply because I had seen it abused."

have little or no idea what is going to happen. Sometimes things will be a little bit "out of control." That is, they will be out of *your*

---

[53]Poloma, p. 77.

control. There will be days when the Holy Spirit will guide your people into new experiences. There will be unexpected manifestations.

At the same time, the other risk is that after you have taught people to have expectations, when you begin to wait on God nothing at all might happen. You can't control this either. You cannot force it. Be patient and let God be in charge. Many leaders do not have the patience to take their people through the desert to the place where they can bloom and grow. Don't give up just before the breakthrough!

Annie: "Your desire for God to move has to be stronger than any embarrassment you may feel if "nothing happens."

The leader must be willing to step back and let God speak through whomever God wishes, yet be strong and clear-headed enough to step forward and give direction and, when necessary, correction. This is one of the reasons why it is good to have multiple leadership in any gathering. If at least two people have prepared together, they can be in eye contact or consult with each other as they discern what God is doing. Was what Jill just shared a prophetic word from God? How should we respond to it? Why do the people not seem to be keeping up with what we had planned? Are we missing something? Should we skip the sermon and go to a time of intercession for our church member who was just diagnosed with cancer?

Reflect: Tell about a time when you have seen a leader deal with a difficult situation in a way that gave you confidence.

The Worship Leader

The previous chapter took us further into the realm of practical application. We especially focused on ministry leaders and their role in helping a church or group grow into an interactive relationship with God. This chapter will focus on the person who in many churches is called the worship leader.

Worship is more than just singing songs

As we continue to discuss the practical side of facilitating a pentecostal/charismatic gathering, let me say one more time that we need to get past this idea that the only way we can worship God is to sing songs to Him. Singing and music are certainly one very important way that human beings use to express their feelings and proclaim truth. But limiting our relationship with God to the one-directional and sometimes superficial action of singing songs will not result in a body of believers who know God deeply.

Mike: "When I sing on Sunday morning, I worship; when I hear the teaching of the word, I worship; when I wash dishes, I worship."

Indeed, because our churches have, to a large extent, drifted into the performance-oriented concert paradigm, we might need to break away from using so much music in order to develop a healthier theology and praxis.

So, even though when I talk about the worship leader, I'm going to start by assuming that, in your current set-up, that person is a musician, I'd like you to begin to think of leading worship as something much broader. The worship leader should be a pastoral person who is deliberately guiding the people of God into interactive relationship with Him. This might include music, but there is oh so much more.

The Musically-Talented Worship Leader

In larger churches and groups (and many of the smaller ones as well), the designated worship leader is normally someone of outstanding musical talent. But this person is not always (indeed, frequently not) someone with a pastoral gifting. Because the typical worship leader is an artist, and because the gathering is planned as if it were a performance, the worship leader will be more concerned with the quality of the music and the success of the planned program than with the question of whether real worship is happening. S/he may also be inexperienced with the manifestations of the Spirit, or uncomfortable with the unpredictability of letting the Holy Spirit have the freedom to impact and change the direction of the gathering.

Above all, I will continue to urge you to move away from the performance focus, and to involve someone with a pastoral gifting and a clear vision for guiding the church into an interactive relationship with God. If the lead musician is not pastoral, another more pastoral leader should be actively involved in guiding the congregation in everything that happens, including the singing. There are many ways to do this, some of which will be suggested below. In fact, I have occasionally—and successfully—placed a non-musician in leadership of musical worship.[54] The goal is, after all, that the people meet with God, that God is revealed. A person with a pastoral or teaching gift is more likely to achieve this goal, whether or not s/he is musically gifted.

Reflect: If you are a worship leader, would you say that your gifting is as an artist, a pastor, or both? What kinds of tension do you experience between these two giftings?

But first of all a few more words to the musically talented leader. Whether you are a singer or an instrumentalist, you have a valuable gift from God and the potential of being used mightily by the Holy Spirit to build up the church. But your talent can also get in the way. Remember that God's people have not gathered to hear you and your team, nor are they there to provide you with a vehicle for displaying your talents. They have come to meet with God. Your priestly ministry is to help that to happen.

Keep the attention off of yourself. Give direction as needed (that is the job of a leader), but don't be long-winded about it. How many times have I seen a congregation whose hearts are turned to God, who are standing and ready to honor God with joyful song or heartfelt prayer. But the leader stands at the front with the microphone and talks and explains and preaches until everyone is sitting down, neutralized, the passion of the moment lost in an overabundance of words. Instruction at the right moment is essential. Words for the sake of hearing your own voice will get in the way of the Spirit and dishearten the people. It is possible to

---

[54] How can a person lead the musical part of worship if they cannot play an instrument or sing? This will be discussed below in the section on the "non-talented" worship leader.

be a strong and effective leader and still have the people scarcely notice that you are there. That should be your goal.

Remember that the people you are leading in song-singing are not as talented as you. If you have a powerful set of lungs and/or a good sound system, plus some musical training, you may be tempted to display your talents. This can be a beautiful thing to do occasionally as a spontaneous response to God, but if you do this most of the time it will simply frustrate those who are not able to follow your "fancy singing." Regular folks cannot sing as high, as low, or as fast as you. Nor can we sing as slowly as you can! It takes some ability to slow a melody down and draw it out. We are left breathless while you are still enjoying yourself. Normally a song should be sung at the tempo

> Dan: "I sometimes stop singing because the songs are hard."

for which it was written. Change the tempo only for a deliberate and temporary reason—for example, to set an emphasis on particular words to which God is calling attention.

Nor are regular folks capable of complicated or "artsy" melodies. Some songs just don't work for corporate worship. Use them occasionally for a special sung or played by an artist.[55] Don't go off on some marvelous musical digression to a place where the

---

[55] I often notice cynicism about "specials," when one person gets up on stage and performs a solo, for example. Sure, it might just be show. But there can be a place for the special. It may be that God has gifted one of the church members, and this person loves to sing or play an instrument or do a dramatic reading, or display a painting as an enrichment for the body and a praise to God. We should encourage such joyful expression of gifts, and applaud those who are willing to share them, just as a family would applaud a child or an adult who performs for everyone's enjoyment. There are also times when one of these gifts is used in a spontaneous manifestation of the Holy Spirit—in other words, God is speaking to us through the gift. This requires not applause but response. Try to discern the meaning of the gift and react appropriately.

congregation can't follow—unless it is a manifestation of the Spirit. Otherwise you will just be showing off and leaving God's people behind.

If yours is the main voice that is coming through the sound system in leading a song, don't sing harmony—the melody needs to be the loudest thing happening, again because the (less musically talented) congregation won't be able to figure out what notes they are supposed to be singing.

Because you are talented, you might love to sing and play music to God for hours. You would wish to fill every moment that you are in charge with musical expression of your love for God. That is entirely fitting with the gift God has given you.[56] But remember that your leadership is supposed to be building the body and equipping the saints. Not everyone is a music-lover. Some of us are desperately yearning for silence,[57] or for readings of the scripture, or for chances to pray and testify—the vehicles that help *us* draw near to and hear from God.

Watch your people, music leader! If you are pastoring the people, why are your eyes closed during the singing? If people are earnestly entering in to the singing or prayer, or waiting intently on God, you need to know that and support it. If they have stopped singing or seem half-hearted, that should impact your follow-up. There may be need to change direction or ask for

---

[56] So find a group of like-minded Jesus lovers to do that with on a regular basis. It is part of who you are.

[57] Speaking of silence, this means ceasing to play *all* the instruments, not continuing to strum a guitar or finger a piano keyboard. Silence is like white space on a page. The total absence of noise allows music to be more meaningful when it returns. So stop it with the Christian elevator music! Let a deep stillness descend on the people. This can be a powerful vehicle for the revelation of God.

feedback. Watching the people will help you to know if the next thing you have planned fits what the Spirit is actually doing.

Being aware of the people will also help you know if there are some logistics that are not working. If you see that most of the members have stopped singing, it may be because you've made the song too hard for them. It may be that the sound level is too loud to hear their own voice singing. It may be that the room is too large

> Kris: "Sometimes worship leaders will add their own 'flair' to a song and I won't be able to follow."

for the number of people, and they are sitting so far apart that they do not feel joined to the body in worship. It may be because the choice of songs does not match the move of the Spirit that is occurring in the midst of God's people. Or it may simply be because it is time to move on. Be aware, be a pastor, be a priest who draws God and people together.

Reflect: Share about some times when the worship leader has helped you to draw closer to God, as well as some examples of when it didn't go so well.

The non-talented worship leader

Frequently the pastors of small ministries, churches, or groups have to lead worship whether they have musical giftings or not. You can do it. In fact, it might be the best thing that could happen to your ministry because you will be forced to find creative ways to help your people meet with God, and will therefore avoid the more routinized patterns that you would otherwise have accepted without further thought. You might have to study harder and find new strategies to make things work, but you could end up being a better worship leader than many who have great musical talent.

Reflect: Is this you? Tell some stories!

Personally, I would have called myself an *anti*-talented worship leader. I play 5 or 6 instruments, all badly. I can't carry a tune. In fact, in first grade I was sent for special lessons with our music teacher, Mrs. Seuss. She made us listen to our voices by cupping a hand from mouth to ear. You will still see me singing that way, trying to stay in tune. Yet because I was forced to find ways for my small ministry in Germany to meet with God, I did more thinking and praying about what it is, exactly, that we are trying to achieve when we gather. And God, who loves irony, gave me grace to be the catalyst for the development of powerful worship gatherings through the years in various places.

Be encouraged. Keep reading for some helps.

Practics—Help Me Learn How to Do This

Preparation for the worship gathering should first of all focus on hearing from the Holy Spirit. What are God's plans for us? What would be the aspect of growing up into the fullness of Messiah that the church should move forward in this week or this month? Do we need to strengthen relationships between people? Do they need teaching on some aspect of theology? Do they need to learn better Bible-study skills? Do we want to search together for God's heart for reaching our neighborhood? Is there an overall theme that the Holy Spirit is working on over a longer period of time, and how will this week's plans support that theme?

After we have some sense of where we are headed, we then ask the strategy questions: If "X" is the goal for this week, what would be the most effective way of attaining that goal? Would people understand and embrace the goal most effectively if we make use of a discussion time or an activity or a sermon? Do we need a guided time of waiting on God with feedback afterward? Are there songs that we can sing or scriptures that we can read that will turn people's hearts and minds in the direction we are sensing from God?

Notice that even though I am encouraging you to be open to the possibility that impulses from the Holy Spirit during the actual gathering might turn all your planning upside-down, I am still a proponent of careful, thoughtful planning.[58] The ability to plan is also a gift from God. The prayerful plans of the leadership team are part of waiting on God. If the team is not hearing any specific instruction from the Holy Spirit, there is nothing wrong with using the brains and the strategic planning abilities with which God has gifted us to organize something that seems right and fitting for where we are and where we think we want to go.

But do not let your plan be lord of the gathering. Be ready for the Holy Spirit to surprise you and take you in a direction that was entirely unanticipated back in the planning process. Talk out loud with the leadership team and with the congregation about this possibility and about our corporate submission to God's wisdom and authority. Indeed, it is wise to discuss and even practice appropriate leadership responses to changes initiated by the Holy Spirit.[59]

> Aaron: "We are afraid that if we let the Holy Spirit do His thing we might fail in our response."

Initial prayer and preparation for the gathering should not be divided up into separate areas—the worship leaders planning the

---

[58] Someone once advised me, "Plan as if there is no Holy Spirit, and enter into the worship gathering as if the Holy Spirit is *all* there is."

[59] The senior pastor could, for example, throw out scenarios: "What if we have planned a time of examining our lives and repentance, but, as we wait on God at the beginning of the gathering, the manifestations and prayers all seem to be along the topic of reaching those who do not know God in our neighborhood? What would you do?" Brainstorming responses ahead of time will give your team more possibilities to choose from, and therefore more confidence to allow God freedom to speak and guide.

singing time, the pastor planning the sermon.[60] Instead have the whole team pray and brainstorm together about everything that could happen—singing, intentional times of waiting on God, teaching, or activities. Pay attention to whether there is a common thread running through the planning of the various parts of the gathering. Try very hard to stay out of performance mode by asking yourselves repeatedly—does what we are planning help us feel more like a family? Is it strengthening our sense of community? Will the people feel empowered and responsible rather than falling into a spectator role?

. One result of good planning is appropriate use of time. There are two important things that the congregation should comprehend. One is that they can trust the leadership to make good and appropriate use of time—the gathering will not drag on and on for no real reason. The other is that there is always a possibility that God will call for a prolonged gathering for a specific purpose.[61] In such cases, people will desire to stay together long past the usual ending time because they can sense the guidance of the Holy Spirit.

But there is a big difference between going longer in response to the revelation of God, and simply wasting time because of poor planning. Agree in the planning meeting as to how much time the

---

[60] This bifurcation is one reason why our gatherings are in such a rut. We only do singing and sermon because each portion of the church leadership is off on his/her own, planning to do what has always been done. It is highly unlikely that any separate member of the leadership team would decide to do something radically different without being able to test and coordinate it with the others.

[61] For this reason, it is not wise for leaders to be apologetic about "going late," or to be constantly referring to the time. As you eliminate the performance mode, the congregation will gradually let go of expectations that the gathering must be finished by a certain time, and most members will stop watching the clock.

various aspects of the gathering should take if things go as intended. Make use of those in the team who are more realistic in their estimations of how long things take. Set up safe-guards to prevent notorious time-wasters from hijacking the plans. The congregation will thank you! Even though you want to be open to the Spirit's moving, you do not want to be guilty of wasting people's time because of poor planning, unclear goals, or inefficiency.

Reflect: Tell about your experiences with good or not-so-good planning, whether as a leader or as a member of a congregation. What have you learned from these experiences?

Pastor the people. God reveals Himself in many ways. He will reveal Himself in the planning process, directly to individual leaders during worship, and through the body of believers when they gather. As you put your plans into action and lead others in worship, you should certainly try to focus on God and fully enter into worship yourself. But, as mentioned above, part of your worship is that you carry a pastoral responsibility for the people. You have the priestly ministry of enabling them to draw closer to God. In fact, since they are participants in God's revelation, if you do not attend to what is happening amongst them, you are likely to miss part of what God is saying.

So your attention needs to be on your people as well. How are they reacting to what you prepared for this gathering? Does it catch them up, or is there resistance? What is God doing in your midst? Are the people stiff, free, joyful, sad, in awe? If they are all down on their knees and speechless before God, that is not the time for a song leader to break out with a happy-clappy dancing song. If folks are bursting with joy and laughter, you would be hurting the Spirit (and out of order) to force them into quietness.

The Spirit guides the whole people of God—or at least He wants to. Stay in touch with what He is doing in the midst of His people.

Reflect: If you are a leader, tell about a time when your plans went out the window as the Holy Spirit guided in a different direction.

Music tips

In a later section, I am going to suggest that making less use of music in Christian gatherings, especially use of instruments and electronics, will help your congregation move away from performance mode. However, music is a soul language for the majority of believers and will always be a significant way of communicating with God, adoring God, and proclaiming truth. For this reason, I would like to speak directly to the musicians for a bit.

Who can be a worship musician?

Whether weekly or occasionally, musicians will be called upon to use their gifts in the priestly ministry of drawing people to God and revealing God's heart and mind to people. This is a sacred duty, and should not be taken lightly. Not everyone is qualified for such ministry.

As with all ministry leaders, musical worship leaders and team members should be in accountable relationships or discipleship groups with other believers who watch over their lives, pray for them, and ask them personal and probing questions. It is shameful enough that the church has, to a large extent, failed to disciple its members to maturity, but the shame is doubled when *leaders* of a ministry are not in ongoing discipleship relationships. With mature believers, this may take the form of peer mentoring or accountability friendships, but no leader will ever reach the point when s/he does not need people speaking into his/her life and watching over him/her.

Be careful about whom you allow to stand up front as part of the musical worship team. The choice should not be done lightly, and most certainly should not be based simply on musical talent. Some churches decide to allow only believers who have reached a certain level of maturity. If a Christian musician is stubbornly refusing to live yielded to God in some area of his/her life, that person does not belong in such a visible position of responsibility. Participation by a rebellious person implicitly states to the others that one does not have to be tenderly focused on Jesus in order to take part in leadership in the church. Remember, the way we "do" church teaches theology to the congregation.

On the other hand, some churches see participation in the worship band as a way of drawing pre-Christians into fellowship and the presence of God. Many unbelieving musicians are hungry for chances to play their instruments, and are happy to associate with talented Christians, even to the point of participating in accountability groups, prayer, and life-style agreements. If you allow pre-Christians to play instruments in worship gatherings, you should do it deliberately, not out of nonchalance. The congregation should be aware that this is happening, and understand the reasoning behind it.

It is important that musicians and worship leaders have a yielded attitude to the overall vision and direction of the church. If you are the main leader of a ministry and have worship leaders working with you, be sure to give them clear direction. Don't just put them in the job and leave them alone with it. Do frequent feedback with them until you feel they have caught the vision and developed their skills sufficiently. Even then, continue to include them in all brainstorming and feedback times. If they are not interested in your feedback they should not be in leadership.

Reflect: What is the policy in your ministry concerning who can play instruments up front? Does it seem to be working well?

At some point you may find your worship leaders taking the vision far beyond anything you were able to do or dream. Be ready to support them as they seek God's heart and find new ways of implementing the church's vision for worship. God's calling on individuals and churches is not static, even if a church carries a long-term vision.[62] You will find that as people join and leave your church, there will be changes in the particular gift-mix of your ministry which will flavor your gatherings uniquely. Practice thoughtful awareness while embracing healthy change.

Reflect: What is the long-term vision of your church? How are you playing a role in carrying it out?

Developing teams and styles

Develop several worship teams if possible, to allow the leaders and musicians to have regular down time. When they are leading worship, and therefore responsible for guiding God's people into His presence, it may be harder for them to enter fully in. Such a rotation will benefit the individual musicians by reducing burn-out and enriching their spiritual lives, but it will also improve the worship quality for everyone. Musicians who regularly worship as normal members of the body will notice aspects from that vantage

---

[62] For example, a long-term vision might be to reach the university next door, to be a sending church for world missions, or to mentor children in the neighborhood. Yet the particular expression of that vision in church gatherings may vary over the years. As a for instance, the world missions focus may move from having missions banquets to facilitating direct cultural experiences provided by members of an immigrant people group who live nearby.

point, whether things that are lacking or need improve-ment, or new possibilities that could be pursued.

Alternating worship leaders will also allow` different styles to emerge. Diversity is a joyful thing in God's kingdom. One team of musicians may love the ancient hymns, while another team may make use of dance and fine arts as a way of enriching the corporate

> Aaron: "Rotation will also take some of the attention away from the leaders."

relationship to God. One team may have members who are more prophetic, while another team may have a deep concern for the development of community, helping God's people to be more aware of each other as they gather in God's presence. These diverse strengths are a great demonstration of the giftedness of the body—the charismata coming to the fore.

But at the same time, encourage leaders to pay attention to what the other team(s) did recently and to try to plug into that. There should be deliberate continuity from gathering to gathering. If one team introduces a new song and it looks like a keeper, a song that will be an ongoing theme for the church, the other team(s) should make a point of learning it and using it as well. If God spoke specifically to the gathering last week, perhaps this week's leadership should plan to carry that topic further by way of response.

Reflect: Was there a song or a theme or something else in your most recent gathering that you are hoping the leadership picks up on and carries forward to the next time you meet?

You will find that most worship gatherings proceed exactly as you have planned them. God has revealed His plans to you as a leader/team. But you must anticipate that God might change your plans, or you won't be ready to hear God's voice when He does speak.

Team leader, be sure you practice enough. It might seem ironic, but spontaneity will be easier and more natural if you have practiced enough to become competent and confident. Go over all the "what ifs" you can think of.

> Jessie: "If you are waiting on God and He responds in a different way, you don't know what to do next."

Your team should be able to switch gears with you without becoming nervous. Practice doing switches with them in the planning meetings, and purposely change the plan on them occasionally in actual worship just to give them experience. Never let them come to think that the plan *must* be followed at all costs.

No one church leader should try to carry too many responsibilities in any particular gathering. If you attempt to both lead worship *and* present a sermon or guide a discussion time, you will end up doing one well and the other poorly, or both with mediocrity. It should be clear by now that it is not biblical for one person to do all of the ministry because this would be to deny the giftedness of the body. In a very small beginning ministry it might be necessary for the pastor to do quite a lot for a while, but even then it would be better to focus on only one thing at a time. Why not use one gathering for mainly teaching, and the next one for mainly worship, rather than doing both poorly every week?

About the songs

Consider the wording of the worship songs you choose. Are you singing songs *about* God (*He is* wonderful)? This would be a testimony or proclamation song, which is one way of worshipping, but less direct. Or are you singing songs *to* God (*You are* wonderful)? This type of song will help people realize that God is present and in relationship with them. Try to prevent the songs you have chosen from switching back and forth between songs *about* God and *to* God. That could be okay for a particular purpose, but should be deliberate, not accidental. Otherwise it will cause those who are singing to have a confused focus.

Does the wording of most of your songs encourage a personal expression of faith (God and me), or is there a good amount of community expressed (God and us)? The pronouns of songs can usually be switched from singular to plural, or vice versa. Either expression can be meaningful and helpful, but again, be deliberate. By being thought-ful about such choices, you will draw people's attention to the significance of the wording.

The tendency in many churches these days is to sing repetitive choruses. These can be good for focusing in on one aspect of God's character, but they also get boring pretty quickly. If you are using a chorus that the church is familiar with, it might be best to sing it only one or two times through and move on. Otherwise, people's minds will disengage, and they will lose their alertness and their focus on God. The only time to sing a chorus over and over would be if the Holy Spirit is emphasizing something. If that is the case, the people will already *want* to keep

> Aaron: *"How about the depth of the lyrics? Are they profound and thought-provoking or are they shallow?"*

singing it. In fact, once your people are mature worshippers who are yielded to the Spirit, you will find that you can't stop them from singing if the Spirit is so leading.

There are a number of outstanding modern hymns and a wealth of ancient ones. This type of song is often the proclamation type, and is helpful for teaching theology, engaging people's minds in their expression of their faith, and even doing spiritual battle by proclaiming truth over a situation. Here, repetition can be good because there is so much depth of content that the worshippers can't embrace all of it the first time through. Worship leaders often make the mistake of singing the verses once and repeating the chorus, when they should be doing the opposite.

Reflect: What types of songs tend to help you to worship most attentively?

Teach ALL your people
how to sing and make a joyful noise

Americans don't know how to sing anymore. We have allowed electronics to make us passive consumers of music. We play worship tapes and Christian radio, we yield to the loud worship band in our gatherings. For this reason, our voices are unpracticed and we lack confidence when we think someone might hear us singing. Even fewer of us are able to sing harmony or play a musical instrument.[63] Since I have a decent sense of rhythm, I frequently bring a tambourine or chicken shake to church, and play it when appropriate to the style of music. But I am pretty much the only person I ever see playing any sort of instrument in the congregation.[64]

> Even as iPods proliferate and background music colonizes the last refuges of silence, from delivery rooms to funeral homes, our generation may be living less musically than any other in history.
>
> After all, when was the last time the fans, rather than Beyoncé Knowles or a barbershop quartet, sang the national anthem at a professional baseball game? The last time that Christmas carolers came to your door? The last time you invited friends to take turns playing the piano and singing after dinner? Only a few decades ago these experiences were not uncommon. Now they seem,

---

[63] This is not a problem in Europe, where electronic music is less prevalent. I don't know if I ever met a European who could not play multiple instruments, sing harmony, and belt out power-songs with their whole hearts.

[64] My wheelchair-bound friend, Mary Jo, is also a passionate chicken shake player.

especially to the young and the urban, faintly absurd. To be sure, music still matters to us. It's just that we have forgotten how to sing.

The great irony is that music itself has made us forget. Professionally produced music, in all its Starbucks-counter abundance, offers an effortless fidelity that our own music can never achieve. There is a big difference between playing a CD and playing a fugue. One is instantly rewarding, the other takes time and patience. One satisfies, the other requires a sacrifice. One is godlike— Yo-Yo Ma or Radiohead play flawlessly at your command—while the other reminds you just how small a creature you are. One is a purchase, the other is a practice.

Andy Crouch in *Live More Musically*[65]

Because our church members have come to rely on others to do their singing for them, it is common to find people moving their mouths to the songs, but barely uttering a sound. In performance mode churches with loud worship bands, many people do not even bother to move their mouths. Look around. If that is happening in your church, your people are almost certainly disengaging from worship. Don't blame them—the very fact that they are still attending means that their hearts are towards God. They *want* to encounter God, but are not being supported, empowered, and equipped by the leadership. Instead of chastising the people, work on changing whatever logistics are hindering them.

Reflect: Does this happen to you? Do you find yourself disengaging from worship? What would help you to stay focused?

---

[65] *Christianity Today;* August 2004, p. 54

A reticence to be musically engaged is due, in large part, to the concert paradigm. People often sing along at pop concerts, but they have come to the concert to hear the professionals, and the professionals are so over-powering that the audience's singing has no effect.[66] As to instruments, if you were to bring your own instrument to a professional concert you would be rebuked or kicked out. No wonder people hesitate to volunteer even light-weight percussion in church gatherings.

So what are we going to do about this? Well, remember how we said that the leaders of the church are there to equip the saints? I often wish that Whoopi Goldberg's character in *Sister Act* would come into my church and walk around listening to us sing and giving us tips, picking out the hidden talents and challenging them to step forward and bless the whole body.

A fully charismatic expression in musical worship will likely take exactly that sort of deliberate coaching. If people are lacking confidence or musical training, Sunday morning should include strategic assistance. Such teaching should not be about "sounding more professional." It should be about having more fun, feeling more adequate as a worshipper, being more deeply moved by the impact of the surrounding community. How satisfying it is to stand among a group of passionate lovers of God who are belting out a song like "I stand, I stand in awe of You!"[67]

---

[66] The exception that proves this rule is when the talent up front shuts down the loud instruments and encourages the audience to sing and/or clap. Such moments demonstrate both that it is the leadership who must create this space, and how powerful the experience of hearing everyone singing together can be for developing community.

[67] There are songs that should be sung sweetly, songs that should be sung joyfully and energetically, and songs that should be practically shouted. Our lack of experience and confidence makes it unlikely that a congregation will be able to differentiate, let alone "belt out" a song that is meant to be sung powerfully.

If we are aiming for something on the order of the jazz band paradigm, in which every person is significant, engaged, and seen as bringing unique gifts to share for the good of all, then it is the leaders who must step forward and coach the people in their gifts. If pastorally gifted leaders are willing to facilitate, teach, and equip, the congregation will grow in ability to worship effectively.

Psalms, hymns, and spiritual songs

There is such a wealth of worship music these days that congregations are often overwhelmed by choice. This wealth can lead to a hodgepodge of thoughtless variety, or it can be seen as a storehouse from which to choose what is best for your church. One aspect of the priestly ministry of a worship artist is research. The musicians of the church should be regularly listening to and practicing both ancient and recent worship music, paying attention to the Spirit's guidance as they seek out and try songs that might be right for the church. Choice of music should be done with an eye to the personality of the church, the guidance of the Spirit, and the threads that seem to be running through the life of the church at any one time period.

This brings us to the concept of "heartsongs of the congregation." There will be certain songs that are just right for your church. You can see evidence of this in how the people embrace these songs with a special fervor. Such songs may be an expression of how their own spirits are answering back to the Spirit of God. They may illustrate something particular that the church is going through. They may be songs that encourage and lift up, or—like many of the Psalms—express a neediness in the church as it goes through hard times.

Reflect: Do you currently have a personal heartsong? Do you recognize one in your church or group?

When you identify a heartsong, use it regularly. For a period of time it will be deeply meaningful and the congregation will love to sing it. But watch as well for the time when it passes into being "just another song," and be ready to change to other songs and focal points as God leads. Avoid the trap of using only old songs that everyone knows because they are easier to sing and play. Songs that have become old can be drawn upon occasionally to underline a theme, but if you use them too much, they will lose their impact, and people will disengage in worship.

Encourage your people to write their own songs. Almost every church will have several people who can either write poetry or compose melodies or both. These are wonderful giftings because they allow the church to make use of songs that were written from within their midst. Even better, doing your own song writing will allow your church to develop songs for special occasions. Back in the early 1980s, Christians in Action University Church had a number of talented songwriters, one result of which was several beautiful blessing songs to sing over people for whom we were praying, including a blessing specifically for women. Often, songs written by members will become heartsongs of the congregation.

Create: Spend your next small group meeting writing a song together. You might try setting one of the Psalms to music or using it as inspiration.

Of course you will need to pastor your songwriters. Have song-writing workshops for the whole church to help discover hidden talents.[68] Explain the different genres of music, and how songs teach theology. Enable your people. Some might need

---

[68] This can make a great focus for an entire Sunday morning gathering, or even several in a row.

courage to make their song public and allow the worship leaders to try it out, but also the flexibility to accept that the musicians may need to change the tune or the wording to make it workable for congregational singing. Others will have to learn that their song just might not fit what the church needs at the time. Not every song will be a keeper.[69] You will find that the quality of the songwriting will improve over time as the church matures.

Other Musical Logistics

Flexibility of technology

If the church leadership is serious about allowing the Holy Spirit to be in charge of all gatherings of God's people, then the logistics of the gathering should support this goal. In the aspect of music, leaders must be prepared for the possibility that a manifestation gift or prayer or scripture reading or the demeanor of the people might make it clear that God is changing the direction of the meeting. In a mature congregation, it will become more and more common that a member may suggest or start singing a song that the music team was not planning to use.

Reflect: Has the Holy Spirit ever brought a song to your mind during worship? Did you ask the congregation to sing it with you? If not, what stopped you?

Song lyrics

In order to be able to obey a Holy Spirit nudge in an unexpected direction, the music team should always have all the

---

[69] Therefore it would be strategic for the whole church to write a supply of songs so that the leadership could choose the most fitting from among them rather than having to reject individual songs that are offered.

overheads or power-point slides, as well as all the chords for every song available at most gatherings. This may take some training of the support people, even a shift in technology, but it is essential if you want to prevent the musical worship apparatus from ruling over the gathering. By having only the words and chords of a pre-planned worship set available, you are in effect saying that this is the only thing God is allowed to do at this time.

Technology can serve, or it can lord it over people.

Remember back when folks would miss Wednesday night church because their favorite TV show was that night? Then along came the VCR and they had no excuse (if they could figure out how to set the recorder). Think about the significance of recent changes in musical worship technology. Back in the day, hymnals and chorus books made all songs available to every member of the congregation, but caused people to look down at the text, and their hands/bodies were not free for movement in worship. Use of overheads helped make it possible for people to be physically free, and—if the worship team was on the ball—all songs could be available in an alphabetized filing system, so that a change in plan was easily accommodated.

The static nature of power point-type worship slides has brought with it a much higher level of difficulty in changing the direction of a meeting.[70] The musicians tend to feel committed to a particular set of songs after they have created the song set for the gathering, and may be uncertain about the slide person's alertness and ability to quickly find and display an unplanned song, or even a planned one out of order. As to these new-fangled photographic and video backgrounds for the song lyrics, they created a sensation

---

[70] Happily, more flexible programs are now being developed and implemented.

when they first came out, but I find them artificial, distracting, and even irritating.

Sound level

This is a matter of heated debate in many churches. Especially the baby boomers and busters, with their love of rock and roll and heavy metal, really love to crank the sound. There are a number of considerations here, not the least of which is health. Hearing *will be* damaged by high decibels. In fact part of the problem is that many leaders, instrumentalists, and sound people already have damaged hearing and are therefore likely to crank it even more in order to enjoy the music themselves. In this case, it is those with damaged hearing who must be challenged to love and responsibility. It cannot possibly be acceptable to raise the sound level for your own enjoyment and thereby damage the hearing of those who up to now have had no hearing loss.[71]

But another important issue here is what the sound level does to our community and our ecclesiology. Music that is always loud and overbearing will teach God's people that less talented human voices are not significant to God and the church. If folks can't hear their neighbors singing, there will be less awareness of community. If they can't hear

Nikki: *"I hate loudness! I can't focus on God at all. It is distracting."*

themselves singing they will often stop, and their personal focus on God will be reduced. In addition, a loud worship band effectively prevents the charismata from coming to the fore in a gathering. There is typically no extended opportunity for God to speak

---

[71] I worry especially for the babies and small children who are often in the gathering during the musical portion of worship. An older child or adult can walk out when it is painful, but the little ones have no recourse.

through the manifestation gifts, and the sense of all God's people bringing those or other gifts to share will be lost.

Yes indeed, sometimes the Holy Spirit leads us in raucous joyful loud worship. At such times (and I hope they are frequent in your church) it is quite appropriate to let loose and raise the sound level temporarily. We want to celebrate whole-heartedly, sometimes singing at the top of our lungs, supported by the instruments, sometimes losing ourselves in the music as we dance before the Lord.[72]

> Chris: "Adolescent boys will only sing if they are sure no one else can hear them."

However, we want to make use of loud music in a deliberate manner and not as the default.

We need to experience musical diversity in our gatherings. It should be possible to enjoy various styles and sound levels, and to be willing to indulge other members of the body whose likes and dislikes are different from ours.[73] The problem arises when one style dominates. If the congregation moves away from perform-ance mode, emphasizes the giftedness of all believers, and places foremost priority on the revelation of God in the gatherings, such dominance will no longer occur because it will be seen as

---

[72] Teens, in particular, seem to need the surrounding, pounding music in order to become physically free in worship. This is related to their stage of maturity, discomfort with their own bodies, and awkwardness in transitioning to adulthood. College and careers pastors, however, often make the mistake of continuing to employ teenie-style worship with their young adults. Some college students find this a comfortable place to tread water spiritually, while others become increasingly frustrated with the lack of depth. In either case, after high school it is time to move toward corporate and individual maturity.

[73] Frequent healthy teaching on diversity with unity is the key to loving tolerance. If you are teaching your people about the value of different styles of worship and about supporting each other as a family, they will be more patient with and even come to enjoy new (or old) ways of worshipping.

inappropriate and dishonoring to God and to the community of God's people.

The internet allows us to find guidance on sound level quickly. One site you may want to visit is www.shurenotes.com/how30/article3.htm. The following is a summary of information found on this and similar sites.

According to the American Academy of Audiology, about 17 million Americans suffer from "nerve deafness"—a hearing loss that results from exposure to loud noise or music. Around 15% of baby boomers, the first generation to crank up the volume, have this type of hearing loss—about the same percentage as their teenage children.

Excessive sound exposure damages hearing by over-stimulating the tiny hair cells within the inner ear. When they are damaged, they no longer transmit sound to the brain. And the damage is permanent since the hair cells do not repair themselves or regenerate. What is excessive sound exposure? The Occupational Safety and Health Administration (OSHA) developed a scale indicating the length of time a person could listen to a given dB sound level before experiencing hearing loss or damage. OSHA regulations permit exposure to 80 dB or less for eight hours a day, 95 dB for four hours a day, 100 dB for two hours, 105 dB for one hour, 110 dB for a half an hour, and 115 dB for less than 15 minutes. A typical rock concert can average between 110 and 120 dB, even in locations with local noise ordinances. 15 minutes at the back of a concert hall where the decibel level is 120 SPL or greater can cause your hearing to be damaged forever.

A good reference point for the typical church would be to try to keep the maximum dB at 80, and the average for the gathering more like 60-75 dB. There can be good reasons to go louder during a time of joyous celebration, but that should be unusual, deliberate, and limited.

Honing skills

I once had a friend say that he was not going to practice his instrument and his leadership skills anymore because he wanted to be led only by the Spirit. While I admire his wish to be Spirit-led, it is necessary to point out several fallacies in this attitude. First of all, it ignores the fact that the gifts God gives us (natural as well as supernatural ones) need to be developed. Just as practice makes you a better piano player, it will also make you better and more effective at pastoral leadership or at a manifestation gift such as discernment of spirits. We should be reminded of the parable of the talents here.

Reflect: We often read the parable of the talents individualistically. Read it together in your group (Mt 25:14-30) and talk about how it can be applied to participation in community.

Not only is practice important for quality, but the goal of the gifted musicians in the church should be to so support the people of God in singing that they barely notice the musicians. This will mean that the musicians are determined not to dominate, but also not to stumble about. You can draw attention to yourself (and away from God) by a display of great talent or by a display of incompetence. We talked above about various aspects of team practice for excellence. Here are a few more.

Pauses and transitions

If the worship leadership allows the musicians to play through their planned set without deliberate times of waiting on God, it will be nearly impossible for the manifestation gifts to reveal God's heart and mind to the gathered people. So you need to take some pauses that will encourage people to listen and respond to God.

However, you want the pauses that occur between songs to be deliberate ones, not just clumsy times of people waiting for musicians to turn pages and get the next song going. Such awkward moments will not invite people to listen to the Spirit, but rather will cause everyone to focus on whether the team is going to get it together. The team needs to practice transitions until they can do them smoothly.

The congregation should be taught that when you pause it is for a reason—now we are going to wait on God. Now we expect God to speak. Silence is not empty, even if nothing audible is said. God speaks as much (or more?) in the quiet times as when the vocal manifestations are operating. Help the people appreciate that silence is full and rich, so that no one feels uncomfortable or that they are expected to "produce" something. The aim is for a servant heart that can act or wait, as the Spirit guides.

Heather: "Leaders can get anxious and fill the space. The Holy Spirit knows what's best. Wait."

I suggested teaching "tidbits" as a part of calling people into worship. However, don't talk before every song. People can think for themselves. They don't need an introduction to the song or an explanation of its connection to the previous one. They don't need the song leader to pray before songs as a way of introducing them. Only talk or pray or read a scripture when the Holy Spirit is directing you to do so, and when *you* are really the person who ought to be doing it. Much of the time a member of the body could pray or talk or read the very same content, and thereby more clearly express the *corporate* call to active participation.

One issue in transitioning smoothly from one song to another is the speed and chords of each song. Have your team memorize the chords to the songs, and then practice changing keys with your team so that they can do it naturally when the situation calls for it. However, it is not always possible to change the key of a song and still keep it sing-able for regular folks. For that reason, you cannot always avoid abrupt changes of key, but learn to transition smoothly even in such cases.

The type of songs that most urgently require the musicians to transition smoothly are the lively celebration or dancing songs. If people are happily singing and moving or dancing, and the musicians stop playing, then take awhile to start a new song, you will lose the momentum and frustrate the worshippers. If you realize that the Holy Spirit is calling for ongoing celebration, and your next song is a slow one, you might be better to replay the energetic one several more times—as long as you see that the people wish to continue.

Growling and squeaking

This might seem counterintuitive, but male song leaders tend to sing too high and female leaders tend to sing too low. Listen to the congregation. If the women are squeaking (or not singing at all), or the men are growling (or not singing at all), then you should adjust the key. The goal is not to have the best musical arrangement for the professionals, but to make it possible for everyone, including the lesser gifted, to sing with their full voices, joyfully and attentively, without the distraction of a song that is difficult to sing.

So, while you want to learn to rely on the Holy Spirit's guidance, you do need to work on skills as well. Such growth in skill and attentiveness to the needs of the congregation will have the result of keeping the attention off of you and will prevent a feeling of awkwardness in the gathering.

Reflect: Write out and then share your current attitude toward musical worship, as well as any creative ideas you can think of to enhance the musical part of your church gatherings.

Ideas to Go
Beyond the Music

So far, the practical tips in this book have assumed the continuation of a more classical use of song-singing as the focal point of a worship gathering. Many churches will want to stop there. However, I'd like to challenge you to consider going beyond the routine, taking a risk to enliven the relationship between God and His people.

Before I present you with some ideas and strategies that might be unfamiliar or surprising, you may want to page back and review the principles and biblical passages that were discussed in the first part of this book. At the very least, you will want to think through the summary once more. We concluded that:

- God still speaks to His people today.
- God's people are like a family—they love each other and like to hang out on a frequent basis.
- All God's people have gifts to share when they come together.
- Some of the gifts that God gives are manifestation gifts— supernatural abilities that reveal God in the midst of His people.

- When God's people gather, they should be expecting God to interact with them in some way, perhaps through the manifestation gifts.
- God's people should use all of their great variety of gifts to build up the whole body of believers.
- When they do that, they build bridges between God and people, thus acting as priests for each other.

Reflect: Are there any of these points that you have difficulty embracing? Explain. Then go over each point together, putting it into your own words, expanding on it, and discussing what the consequences would be for your ministry if you were to move forward in living out these principles corporately.

Remember how we pointed out that having healthy relationships often requires breaking out of old patterns and taking risks? Our discussion of the musical part of the worship gathering has already touched on some ways that a gathering of believers can be pentecostal, charismatic, family, and priests to each other. However, most churches use a formalized "order of service" that is so predictable that the people have become passive and do not feel any sense of responsibility for the gathering. Therefore it may be necessary to take some radical measures in order to break out of the old patterns and strengthen the corporate relationship to God.[74]

------

[74] Humans are creatures of habit. You may think that your church does not have a liturgy, but if I were to ask you what I would experience if I were to visit your church, and you could give me a pretty clear order of elements (for example: opening song, prayer, 15 minutes of singing, ministry response time, announcements, 20 minute sermon, altar time), then your church is following an order of service that is perhaps even less engaging than following a high church liturgy would be. At least the liturgies of most mainline churches were deliberately developed with much theological thought. Many so-called non-liturgical churches follow a pattern that is more accidental than purposeful.

Our goal is not to discard all the beautiful traditions that the church may have developed over its long history with God, but to catch people's attention and imagination, and to fill the traditions with the revelation of God once more.

Each ministry will need to find its own pathway in this adventure, but I would like to toss out some ideas that will open your eyes to possibilities.

Unplug, or even put down those instruments

One of the results of placing the leadership of worship into the hands of musical artists rather than pastors is that American Christians now have little or no awareness that worship can and should involve much more than music and singing. Musicians make music. If you put them in charge you will get music. If you want to broaden the worship expression in your church, and become more pentecostal and charismatic, you may have to move the electronics and instruments into the back seat, at least for a while.

Yes, you heard right. I am suggesting that you put the instruments away for a season and, if your church is small enough, I would also turn off the sound system. Are you still with me? Let me explain.

The typical evangelical church today follows the concert paradigm, and its gatherings are in performance mode.[75] The members of the church have been taught one pattern of behavior that they follow faithfully every week. They are passive, not active, in worship—spectators really. That's all they have ever known and all they expect.

---

[75] Liturgical churches would fit the symphony paradigm better, but the following advice will (with some adjustment) be applicable to them as well.

Pastor, if you teach your people (and you should) about waiting on and responding to God, about being family and priests to each other, and about using the manifestation gifts and other charismata to build up the church, but do not alter any aspects of your gatherings to enable people to grow in these areas, what do you think will happen? There are two common responses to this sort of disconnect.

One possible result is that the congregation will learn to ignore your teachings because your actions do not fit your words. They will not be doing this out of disrespect. They have simply learned that a lot of what the pastor says on Sunday morning seems to have no practical application in their lives, either corporately or individually. Some of them will even breathe a sigh of relief because the things you were talking about were steps into maturity that they are not interested in taking.

On the other hand, those who do listen and embrace mature teaching on being God's people will become frustrated. There is nothing more disheartening than being awakened to hope of improvement or growth in a situation and then having the pastor or other members sabotage the process through stubbornness, fear, or the need to control.

Reflect: When your leaders initiate change, how do you respond? What do you wish for from them? How can you support them, even if you are uncertain about the new ideas?

If you wish to move your congregation to a more direct and interactive relationship with God, you will need to do some things that rock the boat a bit. Because the instruments and musicians tend to be among the most dominant elements of church gatherings, and the most difficult to change, you may find it easier for people to grow and take on responsibility if you remove that influence for awhile.

What can you do if the instruments are given a rest?

- You can work on improving the congregation's singing skills, now that they can actually hear their voices. They can learn to sing more powerfully, to sing harmony, to express the charismata by suggesting songs that the Holy Spirit is putting on their hearts.
- You can create more silent space for waiting on God and responding to Him.
- You will be able to sense more accurately what the Spirit is doing in the midst of the people, and to provide them with guidance right there on the spot without the awkwardness of breaking into the planned performance of the worship band.
- You can do less singing and instead use other forms of worship such as reciting creeds, reading scripture, writing and reading poetry, times of complete silence, using fine arts such as painting and sculpture.
- You can enhance community by using the weekly gathering to eat together, play together, work together, write songs together.
- You can spend expanded time in intercessory prayer. People will gain courage to lead out in songs that support the direction of the prayer because they can no longer relegate initiation of music to the musicians.
- You can give sufficient time to developing important life-skills in your people, such as Bible backgrounds and interpretation, devotional life, interpersonal relationships.
- Again, because you have more time, you can bring in specialists to do workshops on topics such as theology, sexuality, culture, church history, or personal finance.

Reflect: Which things on the list above would you look forward to experiencing in your church gatherings?

It goes without saying that such a radical change will need healthy teaching, both by way of preparation and as an accompaniment during this season of "fasting" from instruments. It will also be important to encourage feedback throughout and especially near the end of this time. What have people learned? What did they miss? What are they hoping will happen next? What are they afraid will happen next? Has their understanding of their own personal responsibility in the gatherings changed, and in what way? Ask the musicians how they experienced this time, and what differences they hope it will make in the future.

The personality and situation of your particular group will inform your focus during a non-instrumental phase. However, the main goal should be that the people learn that instruments and musicians are not necessary for worship. They are there as servants and not as masters. With careful guidance and teaching, people should begin to dispose of the idea that church is a performance to be observed and instead feel a sense of responsibility for their own part in building up the community and revealing God's heart to the whole group.

When the instruments return

Perhaps you will find that this was a crazy idea and be glad to rush back to the old patterns. But if the experiment of unplugging and/or setting instruments aside for a time has been fruitful, you will want to be thoughtful and strategic about incorporating them into your gatherings once more. How can the congregation make use of musicians without the worship pattern becoming routinized again? The answer will vary from church to church, but here are a few thoughts.

You certainly want to consider how routinization occurs in a group of people, and find strategies to counteract that tendency. This will require talking to the entire congregation and asking for their feedback, making sure that the musicians are on the same page, and refusing to drive back into the old ruts.

When I pastored a university ministry in Germany, I found a solution that was helpful. In our leadership meetings we made a tentative plan for the coming month or two,[76] including the "style" of meeting that we would have each week. We decided to allow different aspects of being the body of Christ to emerge in different gatherings. Once or twice a month we had what we called a "classical" gathering, with about 30 minutes of singing, prayer, and waiting on God, and about a 30 minute sermon, plus the additional elements such as announcements that are needed for a family of believers to function.

In the other weeks, we purposely shifted the emphasis away from this familiar pattern. Some weeks we had a whole hour and a half of singing and music, with a short devotional at some point. The music lovers in the group were happy. Other weeks we whole-heartedly sang one song at the start, and then had a workshop on a pertinent subject, thus allowing the speaker to develop the topic more fully and effectively than would have been possible in 30 minutes. Some weeks we spent the whole time playing games, sharing testimonies, or in small group discussions. Several times the whole congregation left our meeting room to pray for the university campus outside. Other weeks we had a Quaker meeting of worship (one hour of pure silence), or one of our leaders who came from a liturgical background guided us through the liturgy of his/her church.

Over time, all the elements of what it means to be God's people came to the fore: making music together, prayer, fellowship, Bible

---

[76] This 1-2 month plan was continually discussed and reviewed as the time progressed. If we realized that the Spirit was taking us in a new direction, we readjusted.

study, life skills, deepening community, evangelism, creativity, etc. But we allowed one or two aspects to have full expression at any one gathering rather than trying to fit them all in each time. This meant that, over time, every element was done with excellence. And it prevented us from getting in a rut.

> Jim: "This makes sense but is rarely done."

Do: Pretend your small group is the leadership team for your church, and brainstorm together to form a plan for the next two months of gatherings. Begin with an assessment of what the body needs and what the Holy Spirit seems to be focused on, then strategize about how to be effective in achieving God's goals for the church.

Ideas to Empower Active Worshippers

After your people become more active worshippers, you won't need to use these strategies—except perhaps as an occasional tune-up. But in order to help them grow into an active corporate relationship with God, the following suggestions may help.

Overcoming inertia

The easiest thing to do in a gathering of any sort is to submit to inertia—to sit passively in straight rows and follow the pattern provided. It takes courage and initiative for a person to break that pattern. In fact, many people will need help from the leadership in overcoming inertia.

By way of example, let's agree that you would really like your people to read aloud from their Bibles during times of waiting on God. You would be surprised how strong the inertia is that prevents people from picking up that book.[77] So, every time the group gathers to meet with God, right at the start of worship, remind them to pick up their Bibles and to *open them*. If they pick the book up and open it up, they are much more likely to be aware of it as a source of praise, petition, wisdom, and admonishment for the congregation. Encourage them to page through their Bibles during times of seeking God, and to share scriptures that express what God is doing or saying.

Do: The next time your small group meets, try using the scripture in the way just described. Afterwards, talk about the experience.

Here is another form of inertia: If people are sitting down, it is hard for them to stand up. So, at whatever point in the gathering you are wanting people to feel free to move about physically, start by having everyone stand. Explain it to them: "You should feel free to sit, stand, kneel, lie down, walk about. But we all know how hard it is to move out of the sitting position, so let's begin by standing, and then you can move to the position that feels most appropriate to you as we seek God together." This leads us to a related subject.

---

[77] It should go without saying that you always have extra Bibles on hand. Let me add a pet peeve at this point. I find it a mistaken practice to put scripture passages on power point slides rather than having people look them up in their own Bibles. It may streamline the process of getting everyone to the passage quickly, but it will cause people to stop bringing their Bibles to church, make it even more likely that they are unfamiliar with the layout of their Bibles, and entirely remove the verses from their scriptural context. This is the opposite of our goal of equipping the saints.

Physical freedom in worship

Some ethnic groups don't have this problem, but North-European white folks can be awfully stiff and awkward in everyday life, let alone when they try to worship God.[78] And even people who are more naturally free and creative can benefit from assistance in expanding their repertoire of movement and expression. You are going to need to strategize ideas to help people grow in this area.

Reflect: Do you feel free to move in worship? Do you wish to become freer than you are?

Have an occasional worship workshop in your weekly large group gathering, during which you invite people to "try out" different types of worship postures. Tell them that becoming a great worshipper is like becoming a great mechanic or a great artist. New skills must be learned and practiced.

For example, choose appropriate songs or scriptures, and read or sing them while people are sitting and then again while they are standing. Then ask for feedback: "How did the change in posture affect your ability to express the meaning of that song/scripture to the Lord?" Repeat this with kneeling, dancing, clapping, etc. Have the congregation discuss what type of worship or interaction with God each posture is helpful for.

Dancing, hmmm. . . . I know that some churches struggle with whether dancing in worship is acceptable, and I do not want to force you into something you may find objectionable. I certainly struggled with it myself, and, because I am not physically adept (a nice way of saying that I am clumsy), I don't often dance in

---

[78] I should know. My ethnic mix is Norwegian/German/British.

worship even now. But I would encourage you to explore Jewish or other folk-type group dances (a great expression of community), worship processions with waving banners,[79] and free movement to worship music such as bouncing (even I can do that one!), swaying, or jigs. More talented dancers can expand on these to their heart's content. [80]

The most beautiful joyous responses to God in my own experience have been at New Year's Eve celebrations of Students for Christ in Germany. Hundreds of young adults from all over the country had gathered for a four-day retreat. As the year switched over at midnight, they looked back in thanksgiving and forward into the new year with expectation of God's goodness by singing boisterously, clapping, and dancing in place while spontaneously formed conga lines of hilariously happy people threaded through the large meeting room. What fun! I know it made God smile.

If you want people to learn to dance, you need toe-tapping music. Many current worship choruses—even those that sing about dancing—are simply not dancing music. You need a melody and an energetic beat that people just can't help responding to, especially in the early days of learning. Maybe tap into some older material or look for bluegrass or salsa melodies to which you can set God-honoring lyrics.[81]

---

[79] Or "Jericho marches" or conga lines. Be creative.

[80] It certainly can occur that an immature or oblivious Christian could dance in a way that is distracting or immodest. This is an issue of leadership and discipleship. Teach, correct, and rebuke if necessary. But do it in a way that does not shut down everyone else.

[81] The best dancing song I've ever experienced is a joyful song called, "Oh Lord I Want To Sing Your Praises," set to the tune of "La Bamba," and used by Students for Christ—Europe for many years. It was so energetic that the moment the music started, people would begin clapping and bouncing and

Do: Have another song-writing session, and this time try coming up with a dancing song by setting your lyrics to a toe-tapping melody.

Giving people a voice

As you begin to teach your people to wait and listen, you will discover that many people are hearing from God, but are anxious about the idea of speaking out loud in the group.[82] Here are ways to give them a voice.

Start with things that are entirely safe. For example, announce that you would like every single person to read 1-2 favorite verses out of the Psalms.[83] Have everyone turn there and give them some quiet reflective time to page around before starting to read. It may be easier to have people read one after another, right down the rows (or around the circle) the first few times, but try not to make that into a pattern. Do *not* pass around a microphone. Using amplification will teach the people that they cannot speak aloud unless they go to a mic. Do not play an instrument while people

---

smiling and laughing. What a marvelous expression of the joy we have in Jesus can be turned loose by songs of this type.

[82] This is again a logical result of the concert paradigm. Would people feel anxious about speaking out loud at a family gathering?

[83] You may have someone in your congregation who is deathly afraid of speaking in public. Hopefully you are aware enough of your people to know who that might be. If so, speak to this person privately and give him/her permission to not take part. If you are uncertain, you can do a general instruction to the whole group that if someone does not wish to read they should just tap the next person to indicate that they want to pass. If someone in the church is illiterate, besides finding a tutor for him/her, you could encourage this person to memorize scripture from recordings, so that s/he builds up a store and has something to share at such times.

are reading from their seats. Not everyone can speak above it.[84]

A feedback time would be a strategic follow-up to these beginner's level scripture readings. Ask the people if a scripture that someone else read spoke to them at this moment in their lives. This will be a tremendous encouragement, as people realize that what they read helped someone else. Make clear to them that they have just performed a priestly ministry.

It is better if people eventually find the courage to step in with a fitting scripture at appropriate moments in the gathering. As a bridge from having everyone read to having people read without being prompted, get in the habit of saying, "While we wait on God, I'd like at least 6 people (or whatever number is fitting) to read scriptures that speak about God's majesty (or love, or grace, or whatever topic you are following). As the congregation matures, they will begin to read out loud the scriptures to which the Holy Spirit guides them.

People who have too much voice

In every congregation there will be people who are instantly ready to share or read a scripture or pray out loud. This can be helpful in the early stages when you are desperately hoping that someone, *anyone* will step out. However, such a person can become a source of irritation or even resentment if s/he always speaks at every opportunity and begins to dominate. There are a number of possible causes for such behavior. This may be a person who actually has a call of God to public speaking or leadership, but

---

[84] I find that if a guitar is strumming while we are listening for God's heart and while someone is speaking, it draws my attention to the instrument instead of to God's voice speaking through the person. And many people who are already shy about speaking out loud in the gathering will not attempt to speak over an instrument.

who has not followed that call or who has had moral/ethical failures that prevent him/her from leadership. This may be a person who is lacking interpersonal skills and either wants attention or does not understand that others are being blocked out by their behavior. Occasionally you may even find someone who is under influence of a demonic spirit and is directly attempting to disrupt the gathering.

In any case, such a "problem person" is the responsibility of the leadership. S/he may simply need instruction and explanation. "Jerry, I notice that you have a soft heart towards God and are able to respond more quickly than most people. That is wonderful, but I'd like you to hold back a little more so that others who are more shy will have time to gather their courage and speak." In other cases, or if the first approach did not work, a gentle rebuke may be necessary. "Linda, we love you and are glad when you take such an active part in worship, but you don't seem to be able to remember to leave space for other people as well. As your pastors, we are going to limit you to praying/speaking/giving a prophecy just one time per meeting/week/month." In extreme cases, the person may need to be rebuked in front of the gathering so that they realize that everyone knows of their restrictions. And in the case of a person who is being influenced by an evil spirit, if there is no sign that the person wishes to be released from this oppression, s/he should be escorted out of the building and sent home under the authority of the lordship of Jesus.

Reflect: How do you feel when your leaders deal well with such situations? And when they don't?

As always, the goal of a pastor should be to provide enough space to set people free to grow and mature while at the same time being strong enough to correct and guide those who need it, and, when necessary, to protect the congregation from disruptive behavior.

Aspects of Waiting on God

Strong leadership

We often think of a strong leader as someone who has everything under control, who is involved in all decisions, and who is up front all the time. But actually, such behavior is a sign of insecurity or lack of trust or an inability to train, equip, and release others. The strongest pastor is the one who can step out of the way of the people, allowing them to listen to God and respond appropriately, and then step back in at the right moment to provide guidance or correction.

Let's take another example from human relationships— parenting this time. Truly strong parents are not the overprotective ones, but the ones who make the decision to guide their children into maturity, accepting the risks for the sake of the end result. Children who are too intensively parented will not gain confidence in their own ability to make decisions and learn to take responsibility for their own lives. Their hovering parents have, in essence, communicated, "I have to take care of you because you are not capable of taking care of yourself." In the same way, pastors who are too hands-on are basically telling their congregation that they don't trust them, that they consider them to be spiritually irresponsible, and that they never expect them to grow to maturity.

I know you don't want to send that message to your church. So, as a strong leader, rather than avoiding risk, you will embrace it. Because you want your people to become responsible adults, you will first take a firm hold on the weekly gatherings and make deliberate space for waiting on God. You will spend time praying and strategizing with your leadership team on how to guide your people into an interactive relationship with God. And you will have as your goal to let go of control as the people mature and embrace their own giftings and callings.

Reflect: If you are a parent, tell some stories about the tension between protecting your children and, on the other hand, allowing them to make mistakes and learn from consequences.

Clarity

As a college professor, I know very well how much communication can be lost between delivery and reception. When you lead your people into a more interactive relationship with God, you will want to be sure that you are clearly explaining the goals and possible results. If you have assumed more foundational understanding than folks actually possess, or if you've explained too quickly or without enough detail, people will feel insecure about what is expected. (Did he want us to pray out loud right now, or are we supposed to wait on God first? What did she mean by "centering on God?") You may end up misinterpreting their hesitance as refusal when they actually would like to move forward, but are not sure what is expected.

On the other hand, you may have explained quite clearly, but, being human, people's minds may have drifted and/or they didn't start listening until halfway through your instructions. As a result, when you enter a time of waiting on God, they may sit there anxiously, wondering exactly what they were supposed to do. Or the more assertive members may do something different from what was intended and the others are disconcerted.

In addition to trying to be clear in your instructions, you might want to use feedback when introducing something new. Ask people to repeat back to you what the plan is. This will let you know whether everyone is on the same page.

Reflect: Tell about a time when you were confused about what was expected of you. How could this confusion have been prevented?

Silence

At the same time, know when to stop talking! Don't continue speaking when you've told the congregation that the plan is to wait on God. Don't be afraid of silence. Silence is like white space on a page—it gives you a break from all the words, cleanses the mind. It also gives relevance, power, and focus to words, allowing them to stand out crisply when they do come.

Americans have avoided silence in recent generations, but postmoderns hunger for it. You may find that church members with a more modernist mindset will be uncomfortable with

> Matt: "We try to drown out the silence because it is uncomfortable—almost deafening."

silence at first, while your more postmodern folks (of any age) will embrace it and thank you.

Reflect: Do you long for silence or wish to avoid it?

Tell people that when the group is waiting on God it is fine if no one speaks at all. Encourage them to relax, quiet their hearts, and settle. They don't have to manufacture anything. God is God. If He wants to speak, He will. And then be quiet yourself. Often the leader continues speaking out of nervousness or a need to control and actually prevents silence from truly occurring. Resist the temptation to play background music, and instead let full silence become a comfortable experience of enjoying the presence of God in your midst.

Wait quietly on God for a good long time, then ask the people what they were sensing. If there is no response, wait some more. If still nothing, initiate a time of praying to God for a closer corporate relationship to Him. As facilitators, listen to the direction that the prayers are taking. You may recognize a leading of the Spirit. Draw people's attention to that and encourage them to continue praying in that direction, to find scriptures that support it, or to suggest songs that would be along the same line.

Over time you will learn to differentiate between the deep silence when the Spirit "settles" on the congregation, and an active silence of expectation. The former will require that you honor God by not speaking, that you wait until this almost tangible presence of the Spirit lifts and releases you. This will be clear from the demeanor of the people as they move from the time of profound quiet, sit up, open their eyes, and begin to look forward to what might happen next.

Jennifer: "When I'm silent, I realize how small I am, and how big God is."

The latter silence is one in which God is already beginning to communicate, but those to whom the Spirit has manifested His message have not yet spoken out loud. There will be people in the congregation with the gift of discernment. If you are uncertain whether to be waiting for a manifestation gift, look to them. They will be motioning you to wait and to expect something more. As leader, you may want to quietly encourage the people at this point by saying something like, "It seems that God is wishing to speak through someone. If you have a thought, a picture, a scripture, a song in your mind right now, it may be part of God's message to us. Go ahead and share it." And then be quiet again to give them time to collect themselves and step out. Your encouragement will help the person to acknowledge that it truly could be God's wish for them to speak out.

Remember, we are steering away from performance mode. That means that it is fine to make mistakes, laugh about them, talk about what is happening, give or ask advice, request feedback. In other words, be *normal*. This is not a spooky thing. God speaks all the time, throughout our days, whether we are aware of Him or not. And there are already people in your ministry who realize this and are used to responding to Him in a natural way. Think of Tevye's bantering and gritty interactions with God in *Fiddler on the Roof*. Encourage such an open attitude in your corporate meetings with God—an honest, down-to-earth relationship.

While you are meeting with God, look around at each other. God is revealed in the scripture, through the manifestation gifts, but also in the body of believers. One or more people may be weeping, grinning, standing with hands upraised, or lying on the ground, all indications of the direction the Spirit is leading. As the group begins to become sensitive to the presence of God in their midst, they will more quickly pick up on the Spirit's theme for that meeting. As always, doing feedback will help people grow in discernment and gain confidence.[85]

Logistics that Help People Meet with God

It is true that Christians should be able to worship God no matter where they are and what the surrounding situation. In fact, sometimes it seems easier to turn our hearts toward God in difficult circumstances than in worship sanctuaries—perhaps

---

[85] It is a good idea to continue to use feedback occasionally even after the congregation has become experienced. There will always be new people, and even the old-timers will benefit from a follow-up discussion that evaluates what has just happened. Ongoing feedback also keeps people in learning mode, humble enough to embrace correction or encouragement.

because we are more aware of our need for God's voice and His lordship when our surroundings are hostile. And of course it is the Holy Spirit who draws us and makes our gatherings ultimately meaningful. He is capable of guiding us into astonishing experiences of His presence and power no matter what the physical environment.

But God has ordained human cooperation in this as in all areas of our spiritual lives. Otherwise why would we expect the musicians to practice their craft and the pastor to use good communication skills? Logistics do make a difference. The way we order our gatherings and our surroundings does affect how people experience God. Let's work through some of these.

How many people come to the gathering?

Different sized gatherings will respond differently to the same physical surroundings. You won't want to approach worship in a discipleship group, Bible study, or even a small church the same as you would do in larger gatherings. You will want to take the dynamics of human interaction and group psychology seriously as you either choose a fitting space for your gatherings or strategize on ways to make the space you have work better.

> Carina: "Studying group dynamics can help you set up your space strategically. Number and placement of chairs can make a difference. So can removing them completely!"

Discuss: Tell about a time when the surroundings made it difficult for a church or group to worship together freely.

If you are sitting in a living room for a Bible study, for example, the soft couches will make it harder for people to stand in worship. If your small group has several members with musical talent and a passion for God, you may experience boisterous singing, but if that particular gifting is not present, then don't try to force it. Your group might learn more freedom with gentle guidance over time, but in many cases it will be better to focus on non-musical forms of interaction with God.

What if you are leading a church plant and there are only ten people attending? You don't want to set up a sound system and fifty chairs in rows, and have the six people who are on the worship team stand up on a stage! This is like "playing dress-up," like little children pretending to be adults. It may be cute when kids do it, but it looks inappropriate and uncomfortable when visitors come into a small church. It communicates that you are not happy with who you are, that you want to be something else, and it will probably make your current members feel guilty

> Blake: "Never confuse the people you're ministering to with the people you wish you were ministering to."

for being few. Visitors will flee such a pressured setting.

No, be who you are. Enjoy this time of more intimate fellowship that will not be possible later. Do a discussion-oriented Bible study instead of a sermon. Sit in a circle, unplug the guitar, wait on God, eat together. Be happy with the people you have, not wishful for more or different people. Show how much you look forward to spending time with them.

At the same time, do not allow a smaller group to become so inward that it causes visitors to feel like outsiders. You can develop strategies to counteract the insider tendency by, for example, continually bringing visitors yourself—even if they are outreach teams or friends from other churches. You can talk about healthy growth with your people so that they strategize with you: "How can we be a happy, comfortable fellowship while at the same time welcoming others?" A group that is comfortable and happy *and* inviting will eventually grow.

Reflect: Tell about a group or church that made you feel welcome as a visitor.

Growing pains

Indeed, belonging to a group that was small and is now entering a growth phase can be traumatic for the original members. They may become nostalgic for the olden days when there was time for everyone to pray at each gathering, and the whole church could come to a game night at the pastor's house. When the church was small, everyone felt important. Now new-comers with leadership giftings are taking on responsibilities that the old-timers used to muddle through.

As you begin to grow, be sure to talk to your older members about this phenomenon of growing pains. Strategize for ways to help them transition, and at the same time be on guard to prevent anyone from sabotaging the healthy changes that need to occur.

Physical environment

Room size. Physical logistics can make a huge difference in the atmosphere of a gathering. If a small group is worshipping in a large room, people may lose the sense of being a community or family, especially if they sit scattered throughout. A too large room takes away the impact even of powerful singing and accentuates that the group is little, causing feelings of inadequacy or even failure when people ought to be enjoying the intimacy of a smaller fellowship.

If you are forced to meet in a room that is too large, strategize on how to make it more cozy and intimate. Block off part of the room with partitions or a curtain, remove the chairs that are not needed, or even have the whole congregation gather on the stage area. One thing that normally does not work well is to wait until everyone has taken seats throughout the room and then request them to all move closer to the front. It is a simple fact of inertia that once people have sat down, you will find it difficult to move them closer to the front and to each other. Instead, plan ahead. Set up exactly as many chairs as the number of people you expect will attend. Have stacked chairs available to add when the set up chairs are almost full.[86]

Reflect: Does your meeting space fit your current church body? Strategize about how to make it work better. Think about goals such as becoming a community, listening to God, feeling free to move in worship.

As a group grows to the point of overflowing their meeting place, a feeling of excitement can result. "God is moving in our midst and we are growing!" But crowded conditions will not work long term. There must be a perspective for the future. The leadership should be talking out loud about plans to deal with the crowded situation, whether it is a new church plant or additional gatherings or a larger meeting space. A too small room will, over time, cause people to stay away: "There is never room for me to sit. They don't need me here."

Seating. We've already mentioned seating arrangements in earlier chapters. This is a much bigger deal than many realize. The way people are seated has a significant effect on their behavior in a

---

[86] It is much better to have to scramble to add seating after the gathering has begun than to have too many chairs set up and therefore a handful of people scattered throughout a room. In the evening gatherings at St Stephens, we had fixed pews, and the participants filled less than half of the seating space. It was my job to stretch a decorative cord across the back section of pews so that people would sit more compactly in the front. This method was less confrontational than trying to personally direct people to seats or asking them to move after they'd sat down. If more people arrived than were expected, it was easy enough to move the cord back several rows.

gathering. One of the reasons that church members are often passive is that they typically sit in straight rows looking at the back of each other's heads. Straight rows cause people to be less active, more "well-behaved." Curved rows continue to reinforce "good behavior," but remind people of the community surrounding them because they can see the faces of others across the room. In other words, people sitting in either straight or curved pews are less likely to take a risk, do something out of the box. They will feel less comfortable turning to pray or enter into a discussion with others. Similarly, theater style seating enhances the performance-audience feel, and causes passivity.

Any sort of fixed seating makes it much more difficult to have small group discussions or family times. It seems a shame to take out beautiful wooden pews in our older churches,[87] but if you have influence over a construction or remodeling project, move-able chairs will be a much wiser choice. They can always be put in

> Blake: "I often put chairs in small clusters before the service, giving me the ability later to say, "Turn to your neighbors and discuss this." It allows me to challenge more people because they are expected to contribute."

straight rows for performances, lectures, or other times when a quieter audience feel is wished. But when you want to have people talking to or praying with each other, unattached chairs will make it easy to match the seating logistics to the goal.

Crooked, haphazard seating causes a feeling of liberty and informality. I discovered this by accident. Students for Christ in

---

[87] One idea for such a church would be to have part of the gathering in the sanctuary, and then move to another area of the church building for group-oriented activities. If you get people up and moving around, you also help them to become more alert, and you will notice that they are talking and laughing on their way to the next phase of the gathering—thus enhancing fellowship.

Koeln, Germany, always met for worship in one of the classrooms of the philosophy building. One night we arrived to find that all the chairs had been pushed into a corner of the room. Rather than set up the normal rows, we flopped down into the chairs as they were, some of the students climbing over top to get to an empty chair in the middle of the mess. The atmosphere was immediately filled with a kind of expectation, humor, and joy. That night we had the freest, most open time with each other and with God that we had had up to that point. Somehow the informality and even goofiness of the set-up was what we needed to release us from some sort of false propriety.

Reflect: Tell some stories about how seating arrangement has affected you—positively or negatively.

Since then, when I am leading a gathering that has moveable chairs, I try to keep the seating arrangement as messy as possible.[88] If there are to be rows, I always curve them as much as possible, and then I walk along and push the chairs out of formation—back and forth, some rows shorter than others. It can help to have a few sofas or soft chairs or tables interspersed among the regular chairs so that the "messiness" of the chairs is less noticeable. This strategy, or variations on it, will normally cause people to be more active in discussion times and in times of responding to God.

I know a number of churches now seat their congregation around tables. They typically combine this with a time of coffee and snacks, and discussion assignments in response to the sermon. When my current church was doing this awhile back, I often found

---

[88] You may have to fight for this. You will find people walking in, noticing that the chairs are not in perfect rows, and deciding to "help you out" by fixing it. They will need to have some explanation of what you are up to.

myself sitting with 4-6 people whom I knew only casually. It was a great chance for us to get to know each other better and become more like family—something we would never have done if we were sitting in rows. Sitting around tables can, however, be somewhat of a challenge for visitors. Be sure to train your people to be inviting to those who look lost when they walk in, not knowing where to sit.

> Nikki: "I love that we sit at tables at my church."

Reflect: If you've been to a church that had people sit around tables, tell what it was like for you.

The spacing of chairs is important as well. Chairs should be placed close enough so people hear each other singing, but not so close that there is no possibility of moving and dancing during worship. Realize that the first row is typically a loss and make it a partial row, placed so close to the front that the second row is really the first.

Room temperature can become a bone of contention,[89] and truly it is important. If the room is too warm, people will be sleepy and lethargic. It will be hard for them to enter ener- getically into singing, let alone clapping

> Aaron: "Even things like the heating arrangement will teach ecclesiology."

or dancing. They will be less likely to be alert when the group waits before God. A too cold room, on the other hand, can be off-

---

[89] I have been in churches where one member would walk into a cold sanctuary and raise the thermostat to 90 degrees, assuming that would somehow cause the room to heat up more quickly. In an hour, the room would be stifling hot, and another disgruntled member would stalk over to the thermostat and lower it to 60. And so they went back and forth.

putting, especially a refrigerated feel during the heat of summer.[90] If possible, open windows and allow a natural breeze through the room to dissipate any stagnant air. Use fans, especially when windows cannot be opened, and if the room is small and full of people.

Reflect: Tell some room temperature stories. Talk about what principles ought to guide the setting of the thermostat.

Location of the worship team

A number of churches have experimented with moving the musical worship team off of the stage, with good results. Sometimes the musicians stand behind the congregation, echoing an arrangement that was common in many churches of the late Middle Ages when the pipe organ, other instruments, and the choir were normally located on the back balcony. Or you might try placing the musicians to one side or aligned with the curve of a circular or half-circular seating pattern. Such set-ups will help to decrease the performance feel while still allowing the instruments to be effective.

Another possibility would be to keep the musicians in the front but have them face forward as part of the congregation, or have

---

[90] I am frequently disappointed by the wasteful attitudes of churches concerning heating and air conditioning. Often the pastors, who are wearing three-piece suits, plunge the temps down to 65 or lower in the summer, making the room inhospitable for their members who arrive in summer clothing. What a poor testimony to visitors who care about the environment. There will never be agreement on the best temperature for a room, so the question should be answered by pointing to the choice that indicates good stewardship of God's creation and the church's finances. Set the thermostat at 68 in winter and 78 in summer, and then put a lock on it! Add in a dose of common sense. If it is winter, we should wear sweaters. If it is summer we should wear lightweight cotton and turn on a few fans.

them face the congregation in much closer proximity and on the same level, not looking down. Churches that wish to maintain more of a symphony paradigm may want to try having the instruments seated in the congregation, perhaps front and center, with the worship leader standing at the front and directing both the musicians and the voices of the people.

Whether the musicians can see the congregation or not, the worship leader must be in a position where s/he is able to observe what God is doing among the people.

Finally, I would strongly encourage churches to experiment with unplugging the instruments. Make use of piano,[91] acoustic guitar and other string instruments, wind instruments, and percussion instruments such as tambourines, chicken shakes, and djembes.[92] Using such instruments could make it more easily possible to have the musicians sit among the people.

Reflect: Have you experienced any variations from the typical arrangement of worship band on a stage in the front? What advantages and disadvantages do you imagine would result from some of the suggestions made here?

---

[91] The large size of the piano requires some experimentation to prevent the pianist from feeling separated from the rest of the congregation. One method that might work well in a small church is to re-create the feeling of standing around a piano in someone's living room.

[92] I have witnessed powerful participatory worship done entirely with percussion instruments.

Help Me Grow!

In the previous three chapters, I've been talking mostly to leaders, while encouraging church members to listen in and add their thoughts by means of the discussion questions. But now I'd like to spend some time talking to the average person who wants to know God better and be an active part of the corporate interactions between God and His people.

If you remember the definitions in the early part of this book, we talked about the words *believe* and *faith*. The first heart issue that you need to deal with is whether you believe. By this I do not mean that you are convinced that there is a God, or even that you have decided it must be true that God still speaks today. I don't mean that you have agreed with the theology taught by your church. I certainly don't mean that you have reached a point where all the questions have been answered. You will have unanswered questions for the rest of your life.

Why won't all the questions be answered? Because faith is about a relationship, not an agreement with a list of theological propositions. You are entering into something like a marriage—a covenant in which God opens His arms and says "Come," and you respond with "I'm coming." Marriage partners spend their whole lives getting to know each other and being surprised by the other person. God can be known, but knowing God is like knowing people, only more so. You will never plumb the depths of God's personality, His wisdom, His compassion. There will be times when God acts (or seems not to act), and it doesn't make sense to you. You will never "figure God out." What God is asking of you is not a seamless theological framework, not perfect behavior, but surrender to a growing relationship of trust and surprise.

Reflect: Can you embrace this description of what it means to enter into a covenant relationship with God? If not, talk about what is holding you back. If so, talk about what your next step of trust might be.

God is calling you to Himself as an individual. He knows you, has loved you from eternity, and wishes that you would come closer. But, even though God calls us to Himself as individuals, God also calls us into the family of believers, into a *body*. We are all separate parts of the body, but we exist as a communion, called to seek God's presence *together*. When we come together, we become the representation of Jesus in this world, and as we seek the heart and mind of Jesus together, we grow closer to Him. If members of the body decline to share their gifts, or even refuse to gather in fellowship with others, they are depriving the body of Christ of some of its ability to reveal God.

God has given you unique giftings to share with the whole body. If you are reading this book, it is pretty likely that you want to learn to share more effectively. You want to experience God's presence more completely. You want to be in a healthy relationship with God and with God's people. Let's talk about some personal strategies for growth.

The first admonishment is to take your time. Four-year-olds don't participate in the soccer World Cup. No one expects them to.

No one looks at a child and says "Why haven't you learned to fly an airplane yet?" Be who you are, be patient with yourself, let the Holy Spirit guide you into steady, happy growth. One small step forward is progress.

I also urge you to talk to your pastor or discipleship leader[93] about your desire to grow closer to God. It is your pastor's job to "equip the saints," that is, to look at your giftings and strategize how to help you grow into them in the context of building up the entire congregation. That might mean encouraging you to step out, but it also might mean working on some discipleship and character issues that are still missing in your life. A world-class soccer player might be left on the bench because s/he won't listen to instruction, doesn't care about teamwork, or is developing harmful habits. Be humble enough to accept the guidance of your leaders, as they humble themselves before God.

Reflect: Is there a discipleship leader or spiritual director already investing in your life? If so, tell how this relationship is helping you to grow. If not, talk about steps you need to take next.

It may be that your church is nothing like what has been described in this book. Sometimes the Holy Spirit does guide us to change churches, but be cautious about this. No church is perfect. You might be overlooking some wonderful aspects about your congregation. Maybe they don't expect God to speak through manifestation gifts in a public setting, but instead the pastor has

---

[93] There will be people in every church who have the gift of mentoring or spiritual direction. Pastors should carefully search such people out and get to know them well enough to be assured of their character and orthodoxy, send them to training opportunities, and encourage the members of their congregation to develop long term mentoring relationships with one of these gifted people.

recognized wise saints in the church with whom s/he consults for assistance in finding God's heart for the people. Maybe there is a strong awareness of the giftedness of God's people in other ways, and the church is truly functioning as a body made of many interconnected parts.[94]

In any case, God might have you in this congregation as someone who can help it grow into a more interactive relationship with God. Set yourself the goal of becoming one of those wise saints, and listen to the Holy Spirit as He shows you ways to have a positive influence, perhaps in a quiet corner, for the sake of building up the body.

On the other hand, let's say you are in a truly pentecostal church, one that takes the time to listen for the voice of God during gatherings. People are being used in the manifestation gifts and the body is maturing into a community of believers who are able to respond appropriately to the revelation of God in their midst. You want to be part of this, but are feeling anxious, shy, uncertain. How to grow?

One thing you can begin with is to learn to *speak out loud*. If you are anxious about your voice being heard, then start with things that are easy and safe. As you notice what some of the

---

[94] One of the most charismatic churches I've ever attended is the Church of Christ in which I grew up in Wisconsin. They have a rather fixed "order of service" for Sunday mornings, and would not likely countenance prophetic utterances or praying out loud in tongues. But gatherings always involve a congregational prayer time in which every person who wishes, including the children, can give a praise report or a prayer request. I have witnessed several relatively long periods of time when this church has been without a pastor, and—though they certainly felt some lack—they continued on seamlessly with community life. Members simply take it for granted that they have a part to play, and are willing to step forward when there is a need. I don't hear urgent language from the pulpit about how the pastoral team needs more "volunteers." Instead, participation is simply part of the ethos.

themes are in the sermon or discussion or singing, try finding a short scripture that fits along with that theme. When the leader invites people to wait on God, don't worry about whether your passage is exactly right. Just read it. See if you get any feedback that will help you learn to discern better and be more confident in the future. If the

> Dan: "We tend to repeat the same prayers or ramble and lose passion."

pastor encourages people to pray out loud, say just a sentence or two. Short prayers are better anyway.

Pay attention to what is going on in the people around you. Does the message you think you are getting from God seem to fit their body language and the spiritual atmosphere?

Ask your leaders for *feedback* after you have participated in a way that is new to you. Be humble and listen to their advice. Be willing to slow down or pull back for a while if they feel you need

> Stacey: "Don't be afraid to be shaped and corrected. It's important for training and growth."

more training and teaching. Talk with other members after the worship time. Worship isn't some sort of magical or private or embarrassing thing—at least it shouldn't be! Discuss what could have been done differently, laugh together about things that go wrong.

Feel free to *use your brain!* Just because we are trying to make room for God to speak in our midst doesn't mean that our minds will be bypassed. God made your brain. God can give you ideas that fit right in, and you might not feel any kind of emotion with it. But be careful that you do not rely on your brain to the exclusion of the other parts of you.

Feel free to *use your emotions!* It is okay to weep in front of others as God shows His own deep anguish about a situation, to express frustration by stamping your foot, to speak loudly when rebuking satan, to laugh and dance when God's joy floods through you. But be careful that you do not rely on your emotions to the exclusion of the other parts of you.

Reflect: Do you tend to be a "brain person" or an "emotion person"? How can you begin to balance things out so that your whole person is taking part in worship?

Make mistakes. Make as many mistakes as possible. It is like learning to ride a horse. If you fall off enough times you will gain the security needed to be a relaxed and confident rider. Or like learning a language—if you chatter away in your baby talk, making silly mistakes and amusing the natives, you will eventually master the language. If you are stiff and anxious that you might say something embarrassing, you will never master it. In the same way, if you make mistakes often enough while participating in worship,

> Aaron: "We're concerned about being all put together for those around us."

you won't mind so much. Your pride will have less power over you.

Discuss and Pray: As you come to the end of your corporate study of these simple concepts about what it means to be God's gathered people, list off the things that you have learned, the things that trouble you, the things that you are looking forward to. Be accountable to each other for individual and group progress, and pray for the Holy Spirit to come, to guide, and to manifest the heart of God in your gatherings.

Epilogue

This is not the end of the story. The very manner of God's interaction with human beings determines that there will always be more to learn and experience. We are here, you and I, somewhere in the middle of God's redemption history, writing our part of the magnificent tale of the God who speaks and the people who listen.

For this reason, I have designed *When You Come Together* to be a catalyst, not a final word. There were many years of learning, experiencing, teaching, and formulating that went before. God's people who read the words on these pages will agree, disagree, experiment, and develop in their relationship to God and their understanding of Him. Church leadership teams, small group Bible studies, and whole churches will write their own chapters.

To further the catalyst function of *When You Come Together*, I have created a website, **www.beingchurch.com**, in order to provide another space for ongoing discussion. There are several ways in which you can take part:

1. You can visit the website and meet other people there who are earnestly seeking the heart of God. Let's pray for each other and share comments and questions.

2. In the following pages, you will find a basic bibliography. These are books and some other resources that have impacted my own life and challenged me to grow and develop in my understanding of what it means to be the people of God. However, I am sure that I will discover more resources in coming years, and you also will have your own suggestions. I'd like to invite you to submit them to be added to the ever expanding list on the website.

3. The website will also contain several suggestions for where you can find similar conversations, as well as contact information to reach me personally for consultation.

I hope that you will gather with others to seek God earnestly, to listen and respond to His voice, and to share your gifts in order to build up God's church.

Bibliography

Bible Study

Fee, Gordon D. & Douglas Stuart, *How to Read the Bible for All Its Worth,* *2nd ed*; Grand Rapids: Zondervan Publishing House, 1981. There are other books on how to correctly handle scripture, but Fee and Stuart have produced a clear, user-friendly book that can't be beat.

Learning to Respond to God

Foster, Richard J., *Celebration of Discipline: The Path to Spiritual Growth, 3rd ed*; San Francisco: Harper & Row Publishers, 1988. A charismatic Quaker, Foster is a master of making the devotional life come alive. Read everything he writes.

Foster, Richard J., *Freedom of Simplicity: Finding Harmony in a Complex World*; Cambridge: Harper & Row Publishers, 2005.

Foster, Richard J., *The Challenge of the Disciplined Life: Money, Sex, Power*; New York: HarperCollins Publishers, 1985.

Frodsham, Stanley Howard, *Smith Wigglesworth: Apostle of Faith*; Springfield, MO: Gospel Publishing House, 1973. Learning to live by faith.

Geegh, Mary, *God Guides*. A 50 page booklet packed with assistance and inspiration for people who wish to learn how to wait on and hear from God. Distributed by Pray America, P.O. Box 14070, Lansing, MI 48901.

Lawrence, Brother, *The Practice of the Presence of God;* Grand Rapids, MI: Spire Books, 1967. Brother Lawrence lived with the goal of constant awareness of God's presence.

Peterson, Eugene H., *Subversive Spirituality;* Grand Rapids: Wm B. Eedermans Co., 1997. Peterson is always good for life with God. He is especially attractive to more intellectually-oriented folks who want to use their minds in response to God.

Peterson, Eugene H., *The Contemplative Pastor: Returning to the Art of Spiritual Direction;* Grand Rapids, MI: Wm B. Eerdmans Publishing Co., 1993

Quaker Worship: The following website can provide you with some hints on trying an hour of silence in the Quaker tradition. I've found it best to make a printed explanatory handout that can be given to each person as they enter. This is especially helpful for visitors. http://www.quakerinfo.org/quakerism/worship.html

Quinn, Robert E., *Deep Change: Discovering the Leader Within;* San Francisco: Jossey-Bass Publishers, 1996. This book is not about encountering God, but about how people change, which makes it a good fit in this topic, since encountering God should lead to inner change.

Wilkerson, David., *The Cross and the Switchblade;* New Jersey: Spire Books, 1963. A great pentecostal example of a man who listened to God, responded in obedience to God's surprising instructions, and saw a great ministry develop as a result.

Ecclesiology (Church)

Anderson, Leith, *A Church for the 21st Century;* Minneapolis: Bethany House Publishers, 1992.

Banks, Robert, *Paul's Idea of Community,* rev. ed.; Peabody, MA: Hendrickson Publishers, 1994.

Bonhoeffer, Dietrich, *Life Together: A Discussion of Christian Fellowship;* New York: Harper and Row Publishers, 1954.

Bibliography

Bonhoeffer, Dietrich, *The Cost Of Discipleship;* New York: Macmillan Publishing Co., 1963.

Brunner, Emil, *The Misunderstanding of the Church;* Cambridge: Lutterworth Press, 1952.

Coleman, Robert E., *The Master Plan of Evangelism,* 2nd ed.; Grand Rapids, MI: Revell, 1993. A small book with a big message: that the way Jesus intends to reach the world is not through mass evangelism but through the discipling of the nations.

Donovan, Vincent J., *Christianity Rediscovered,* 25th anniversary ed.; Maryknoll, NY: Orbis Books, 2003. A marvelous story of building the church in a new culture, and thereby coming to understand better what the church was meant to be. If you only read one book, make it this one.

Hybels, Bill and Mark Mittelberg, *Becoming a Contagious Christian: Communicating Your Faith in a Style that Fits You;* Grand Rapids, MI: Zondervan Publishing House, 2007.

Kraft, Charles H., *Communication Theory for Christian Witness;* Maryknoll, NY: Orbis Books, 1991. The limitations of the sermon for changing lives, and how to improve on it.

Kraus, C. Norman, *The Community of the Spirit: How the Church Is in the World;* Scottdale, PA: Herald Press, 1993.

Ladd, George, E., *The Gospel of the Kingdom: Scriptural Studies in the Kingdom of God;* Grand Rapids, MI: Wm. B. Eerdmans Publishing Co., 1959.

Ogden, Greg, *The New Reformation: Returning the Ministry to the People of God;* Grand Rapids, MI: Zondervan Publishing House, 1990. A strong argument for liberating the laity to do the work of the ministry.

Peterson, Jim, *Church without Walls: Moving Beyond Traditional Boundaries;* Colorado Springs: Navpress, 1992.

Peterson, Jim, *Lifestyle Discipleship: The Challenge of Following Jesus in Today's World;* Colorado Springs: Navpress, 1993.

Peterson, Jim, *Living Proof: Sharing the Gospel Naturally,* 2nd ed.; Colorado Springs: NavPress, 1988.

Sjogren, Steve, *Conspiracy of Kindness;* Ann Arbor, MI: Servant Publications, 1993.

Slaughter, Michael, *UnLearning Church: Just When You Thought You Had Leadership all Figured Out!;* Loveland, CO: Group Publishing, 2002.

Snyder, Howard A., *Liberating the Church: The Ecology of Church and Kingdom;* Downers Grove, IL: Inter Varsity Press, 1983.

Snyder, Howard A., *The Community of the King,* rev. ed.; Downers Grove, IL: Inter Varsity Press, 2004. Snyder's books feel a little dated, but no one has understood the essence of the church better than he has. Read everything he has written, but especially this one.

Snyder, Howard A., *The Problem of Wine Skins: Church Structure in a Technological Age;* Downers Grove, IL: Inter Varsity Press, 1975.

Stafford, Tim, *The Friendship Gap: Reaching Out Across Cultures;* Downers Grove, IL: Inter Varsity Press, 1984.

Van Engen, Charles, *God's Missionary People: Rethinking the Purpose of the Local Church;* Grand Rapids, MI: Baker Book House, 1991.

Van Engen, Charles, *The Uniqueness of Christ: Shaping Faith and Mission;* Charles Van Engen Pub: 1996.

Van Engen, Charles, *You Are My Witnesses: Drawing from Your Spiritual Journey to Evangelize Your Neighbors;* Eugene, OR: Wipf and Stock Publishers, 2009.

Pneumatology (Holy Spirit)

Fee, Gordon D., *God's Empowering Presence: the Holy Spirit in the Letters of Paul;* Hendrickson's Publishers, 1994. A dense theological lifework of a great Pentecostal scholar.

Fee, Gordon D., *Paul, the Spirit and the People of God;* Hendrickson Publishers, 1996. A distillation of *God's Empowering Presence* that is easier to read as a non-academic.

Green, Michael, *I Believe in the Holy Spirit,* rev. ed.; Grand Rapids: Wm B. Eerdmans Publishing Co., 2004.

Bibliography

Pentecostal and Charismatic Movements

I'm afraid this list is rather focused on the American manifestations of these movements. I hope others will add to this list online. However, for an extensive bibliography of the global Pentecostal/Charismatic movement, see Allan Anderson's website: http://artsweb.bham.ac.uk/aanderson/index.htm

Blumhoffer, Edith L., *Aimee Semple McPherson: Everybody's Sister;* Grand Rapids: Wm. B. Eerdmans Publishing Co., 1993.

Blumhoffer, Edith L., *Restoring the Faith: The Assemblies of God, Pentecostalism, and American Culture;* Chicago: University of Illinois Press, 1993.

Goff, James R. Jr., *Fields White Unto Harvest;* Fayetteville: The University of Arkansas Press, 1988.

Menzies, William W., *Anointed to Serve;* Springfield, MO: Gospel Publishing House, 1971.

Palmer, Phoebe., *The Way Of Holiness;* Salem: Schmul Publishing Co., Inc., 1988. (This appears to be a reprint.)

Parham, Sarah, *The Life of Charles F. Parham: Founder of the Apostolic Faith Movement;* Baxter Springs, KS: Apostolic Faith Bible College, c1930. Written by his wife, this may be a difficult book to locate. Try interlibrary loan, or the library of a Pentecostal college.

Poloma, Margaret M., *The Assemblies of God at the Crossroads: Charisma and Institutional Dilemmas;* Knoxville: The University of Tennessee Press, 1989.

Robeck, Cecil M. Jr., *The Azusa Street Mission and Revival: The Birth of the Global Pentecostal Movement;* Nashville: Thomas Nelson, 2006.

Snyder, Howard A., *Signs of the Spirit: How God Reshapes the Church;* Eugene, OR: Wipf and Stock Publishers, 1997.

Snyder, Howard A., *The Divided Flame: Wesleyans and the Charismatic Renewal;* Grand Rapids, MI: Francis Asbury Press of Zondervan Publishing House, 1986.

Suenens, Léon Joseph Cardinal, *Ecumenism and Charismatic Renewal: Theological and Pastoral Orientations;* Southbend: Servant Books, 1978.

Suenens, Léon Joseph Cardinal, *A New Pentecost?;* New York: Seabury Press, 1975.

Synan, Vinson, *The Holiness-Pentecostal Movement in the United States;* Grand Rapids: Wm B. Eerdmans Publishing Co., 1971.

Synan, Vinson, *The Holiness-Pentecostal Tradition: Charismatic Movements in the Twentieth Century;* Grand Rapids: Wm. B. Eerdmans Publishing Co., 1997.

Responses to Emerging Culture

Because Western culture is so fluid, these books tend to be relevant for only a few years. Better to borrow than to buy.

Creps, Earl. Earl is a great source of information and keeps up with the moving target of cultural changes. He is currently planting a church in Berkeley. See all of his books and resources at http://www.earlcreps.com/

Everts, Don, *Jesus with Dirty Feet: A Down-to-Earth Look at Christianity for the Curious and Skeptical;* Downers Grove, IL: Inter Varsity Press, 1999.

Frost, Michael, *Exiles: Living Missionally in a Post-Christian Culture;* Peabody, MA: Hendrickson Publishers, 2006.

Frost, Michael and Hirsch, Alan, *The Shaping of Things to Come: Innovation and Mission for the 21st-Century Church;* Peabody, MA: Hendrickson Publishers, 2003.

Gibbs, Eddie and Bolger, Ryan K., *Emerging Churches: Creating Christian Community in Postmodern Cultures;* Grand Rapids, MI: Baker Book House, 2005.

Hunter, George G. III, *How to Reach Secular People;* Nashville, TN: Abingdon Press, 1992.

Kimball, Dan, *The Emerging Church: Vintage Christianity for New Generations;* Grand Rapids, MI: Zondervan, 2003.

Bibliography

Kimball, Dan, *Emerging Worship: Creating Worship Gatherings for New Generations;* Grand Rapids, MI: Zondervan, 2004.

Long, Jimmy, *Generating Hope: A Strategy for Reaching the Postmodern Generation;* London: Marshall Pickering, 1997.

McLaren, Brian D., *More Ready Than You Realize: Evangelism as Dance in the Postmodern Matrix;* Grand Rapids, MI: Zondervan, 2002. I know McLaren's more recent stuff is theologically suspect, but he did a masterful job of describing and responding to emerging culture in his earlier works.

McLaren, Brian D., *A New Kind of Christian: A Tale of Two Friends on a Spiritual Journey;* San Francisco: Jossey-Bass Pub, 2001. This book helped a number of my friends stay in the church even when they were on the verge of leaving out of frustration.

Index

About the Author

Dr. Amy Anderson shares a home with three cats in St Paul, Minnesota, in an inner-city, multi-ethnic neighborhood. She has been a dairy farm manager, a veterinary assistant, and a missionary to German universities. Having grown up on a farm, she loves to be outdoors—whether in her garden or camping and hiking. After completing her PhD at the University of Birmingham, England, Dr. Amy became Professor of Greek and New Testament at North Central University. She frequently has current and former students in her home for German breakfasts, British Cream Teas, and Charlie parties (you will have to ask about that one). In recent years, Dr. Amy also earned the titles "Mom" and "Grandma," an experience that has taught her all sorts of lessons about God's sacrificial love.